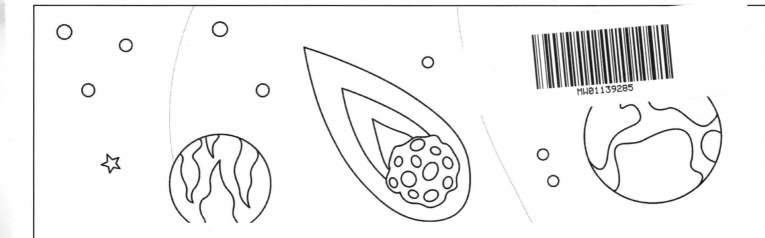

Space
Coloring Book
for Kids

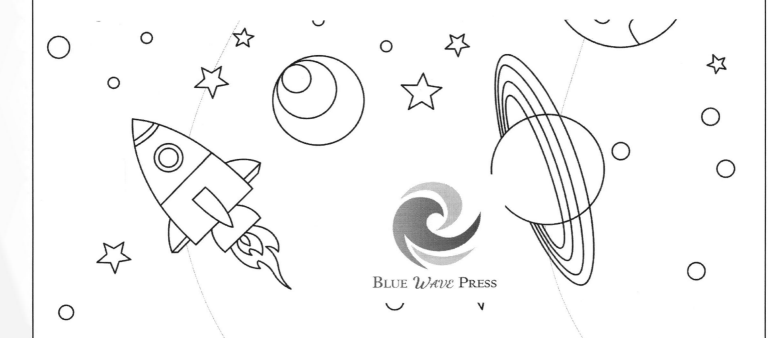

BLUE WAVE PRESS

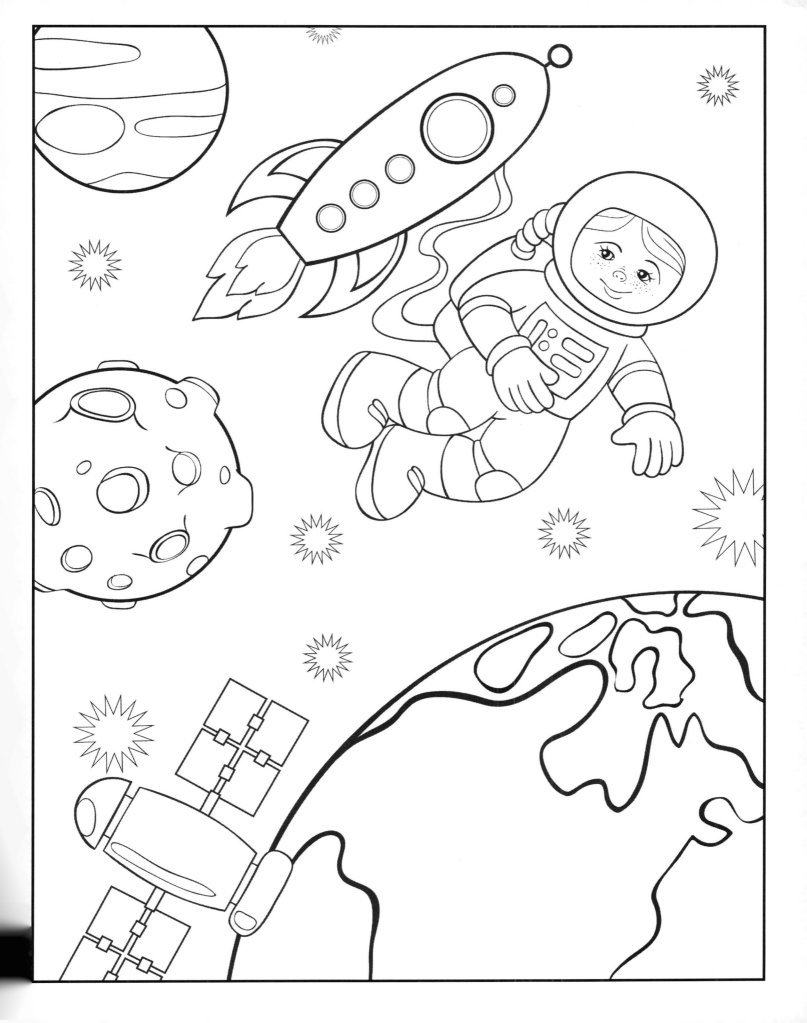

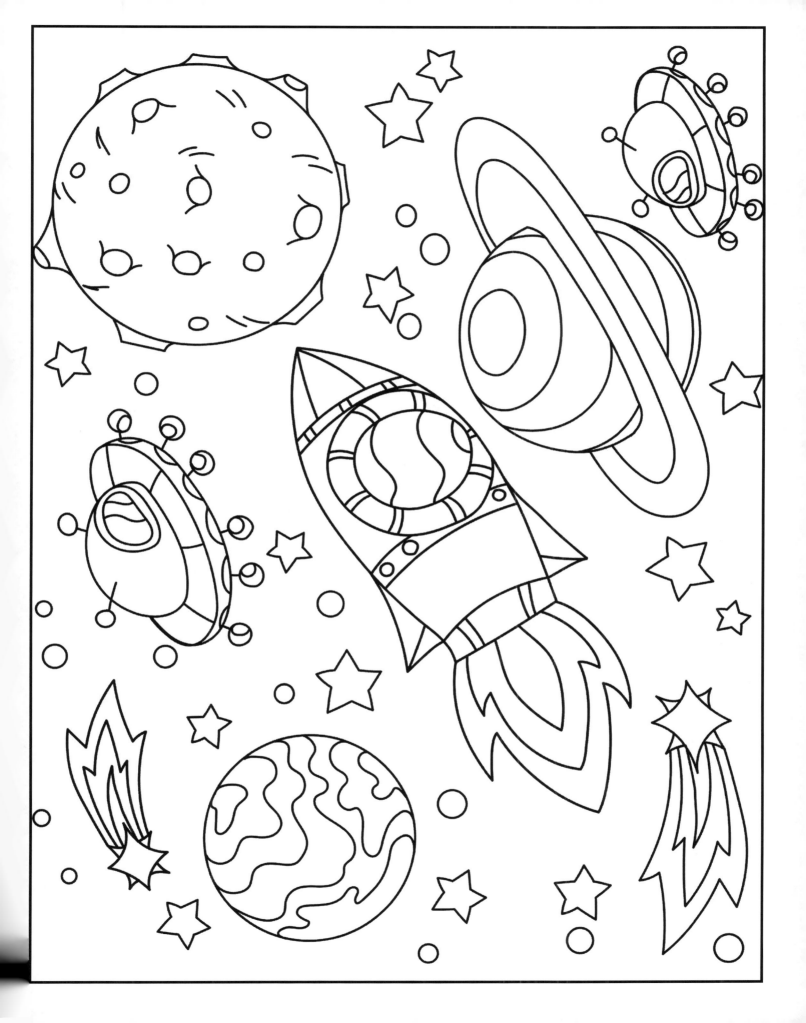

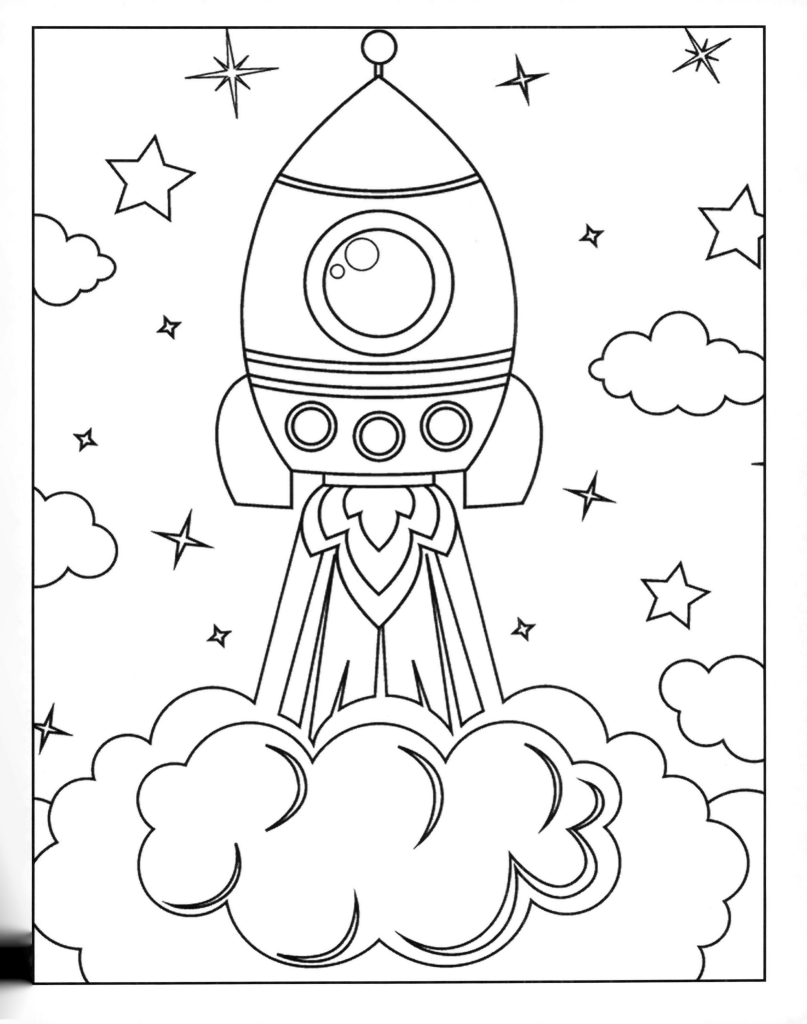

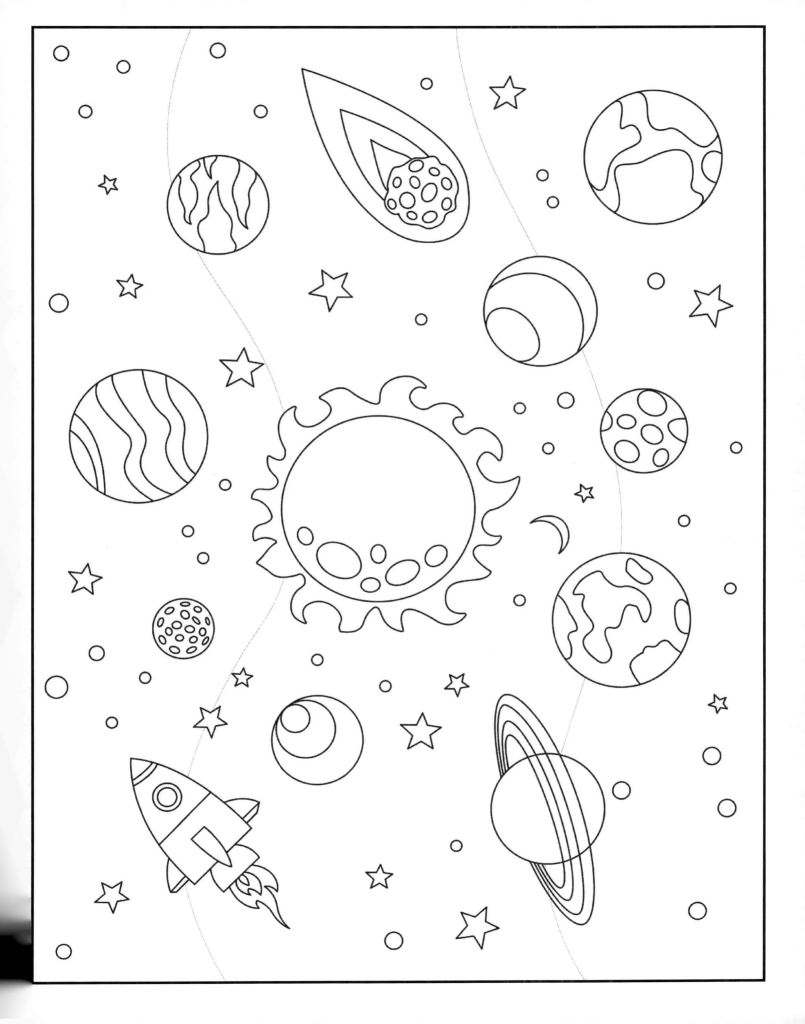

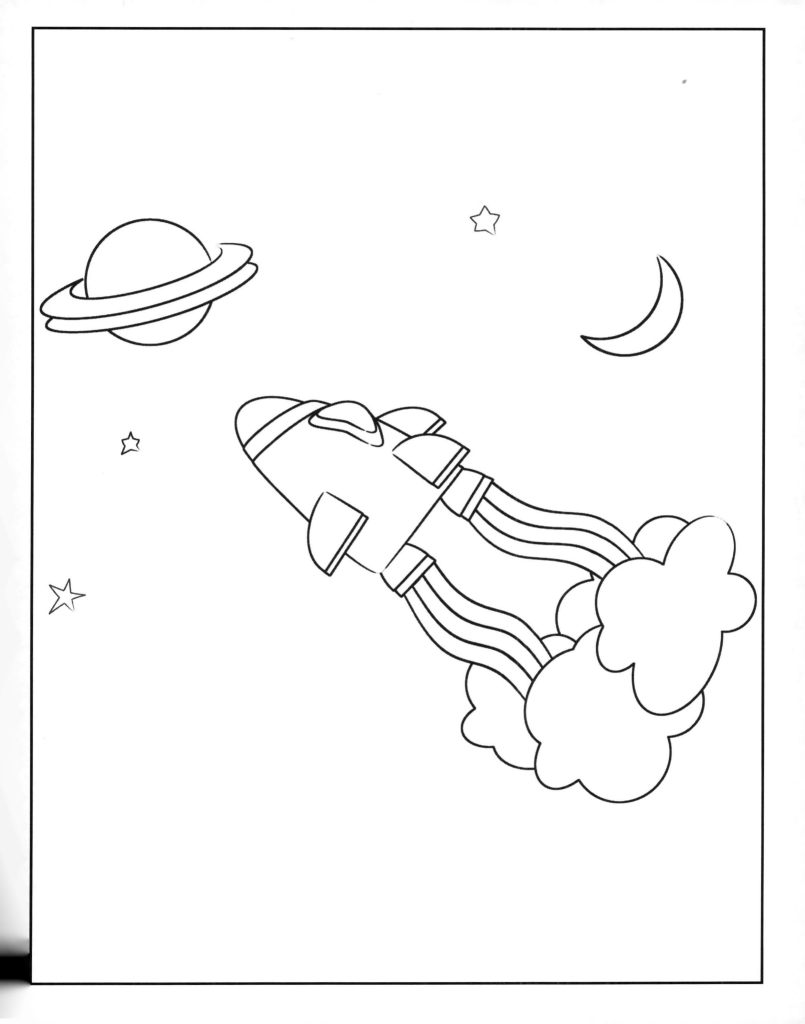

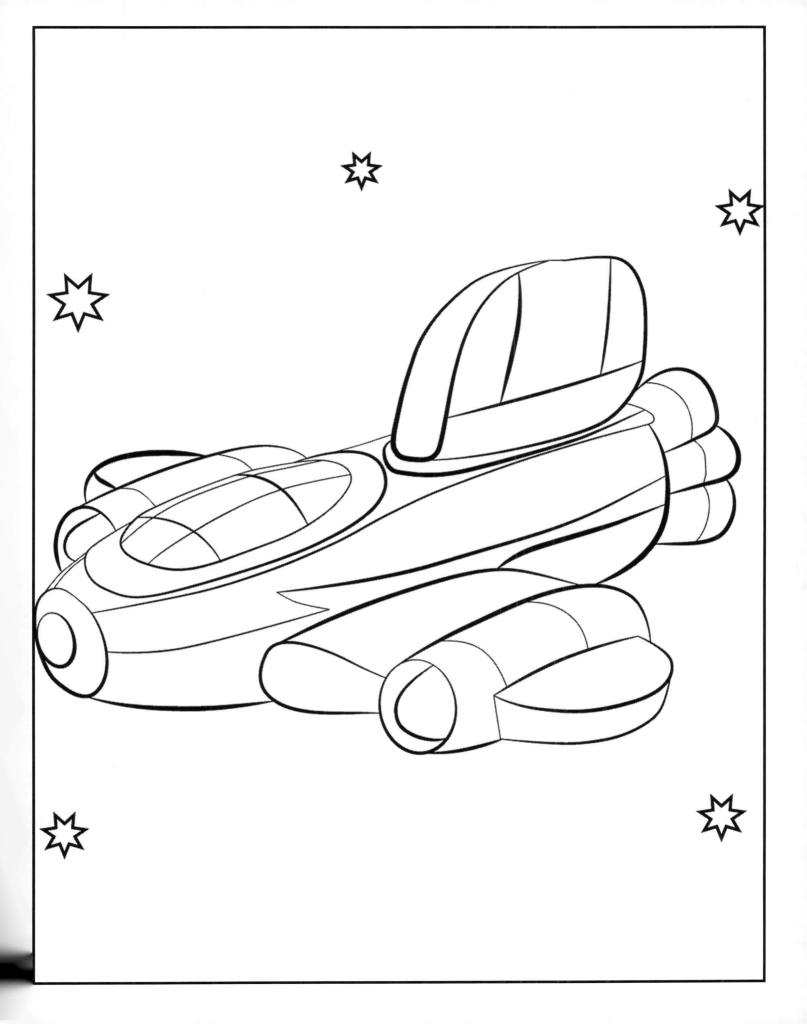

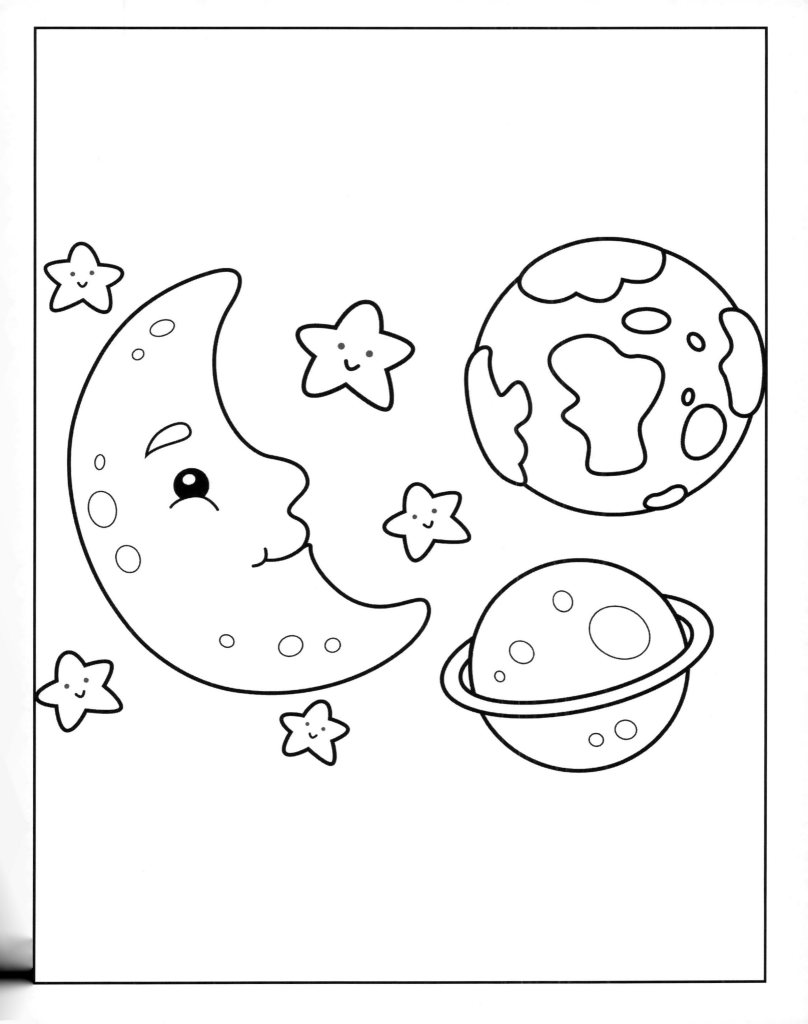

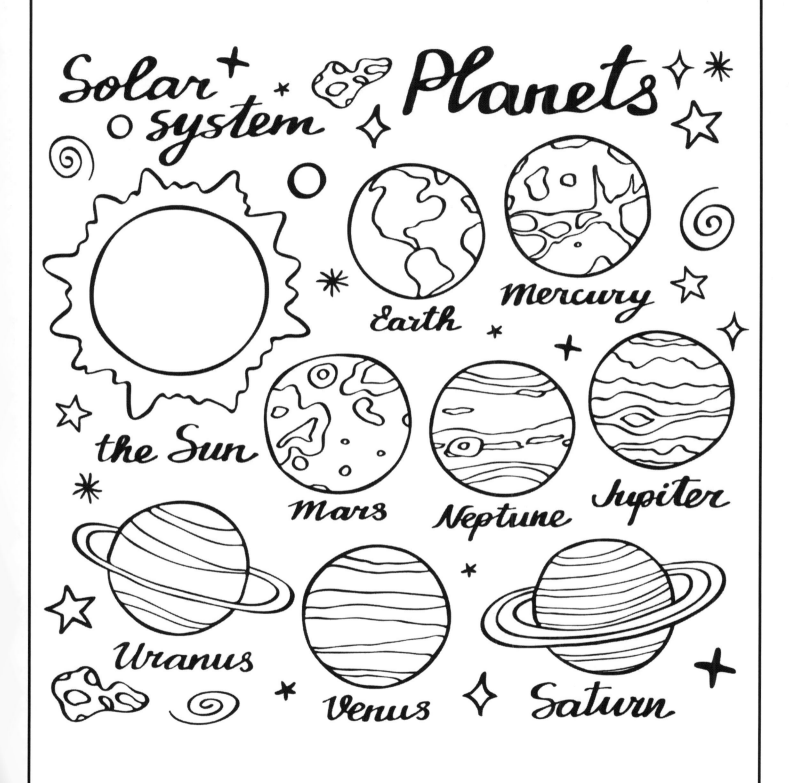

Solar + system Planets

the Sun

Earth

Mercury

Mars

Neptune

Jupiter

Uranus

Venus

Saturn

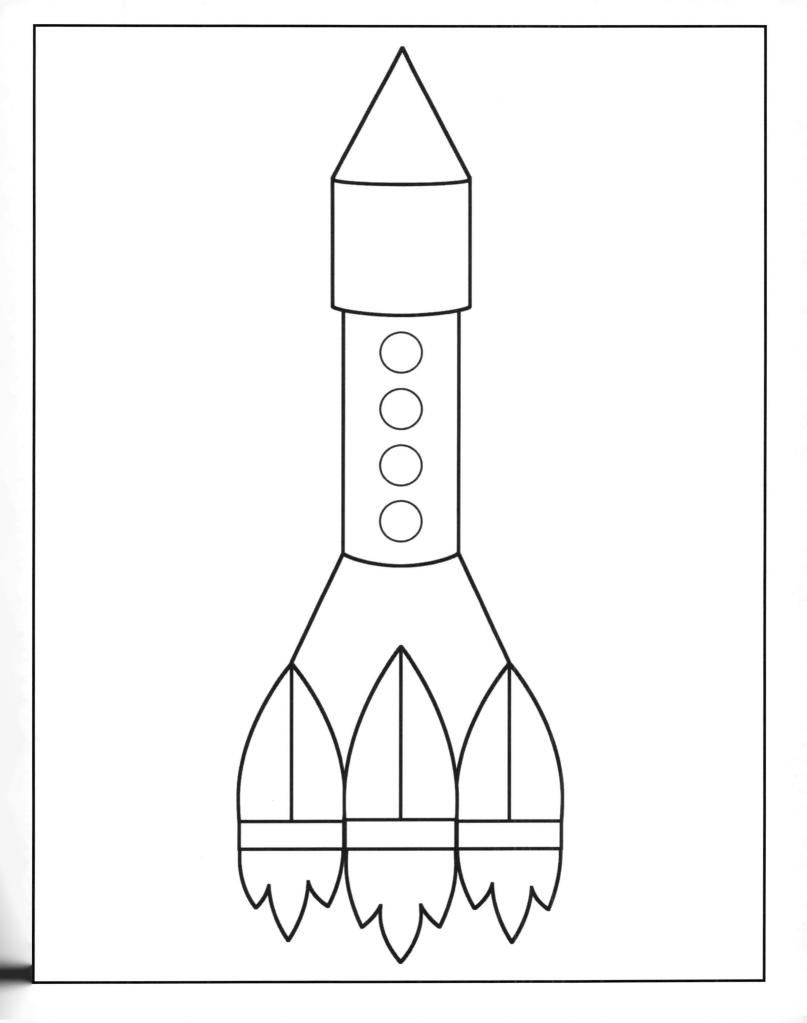

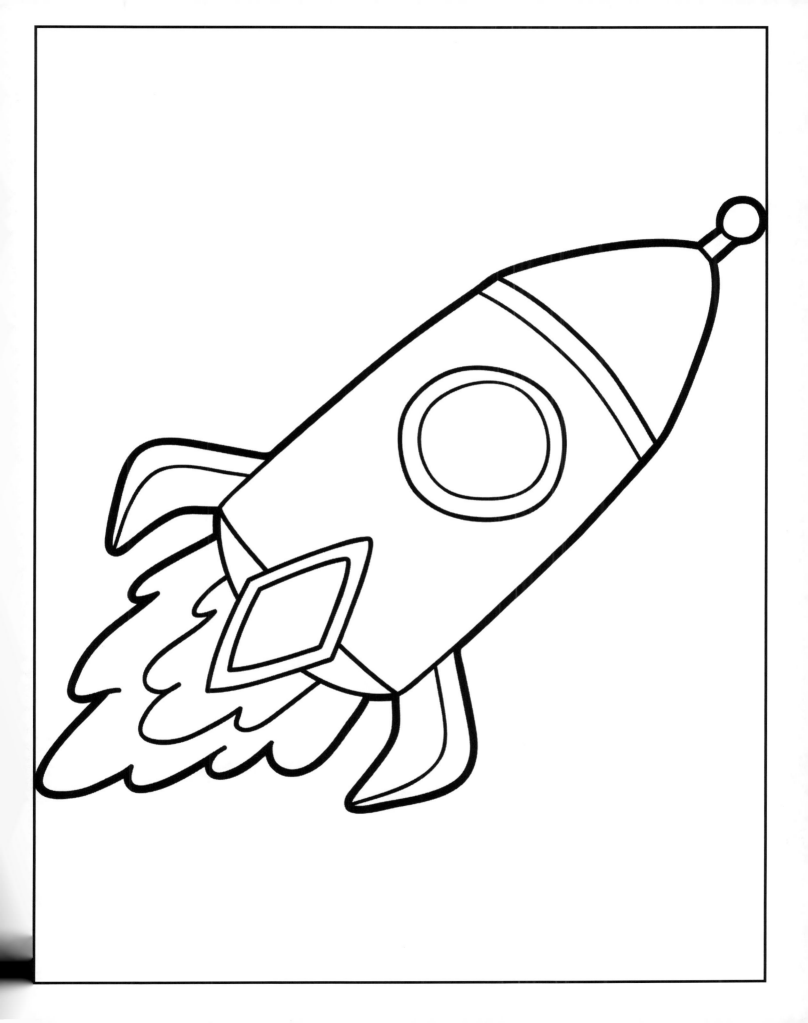

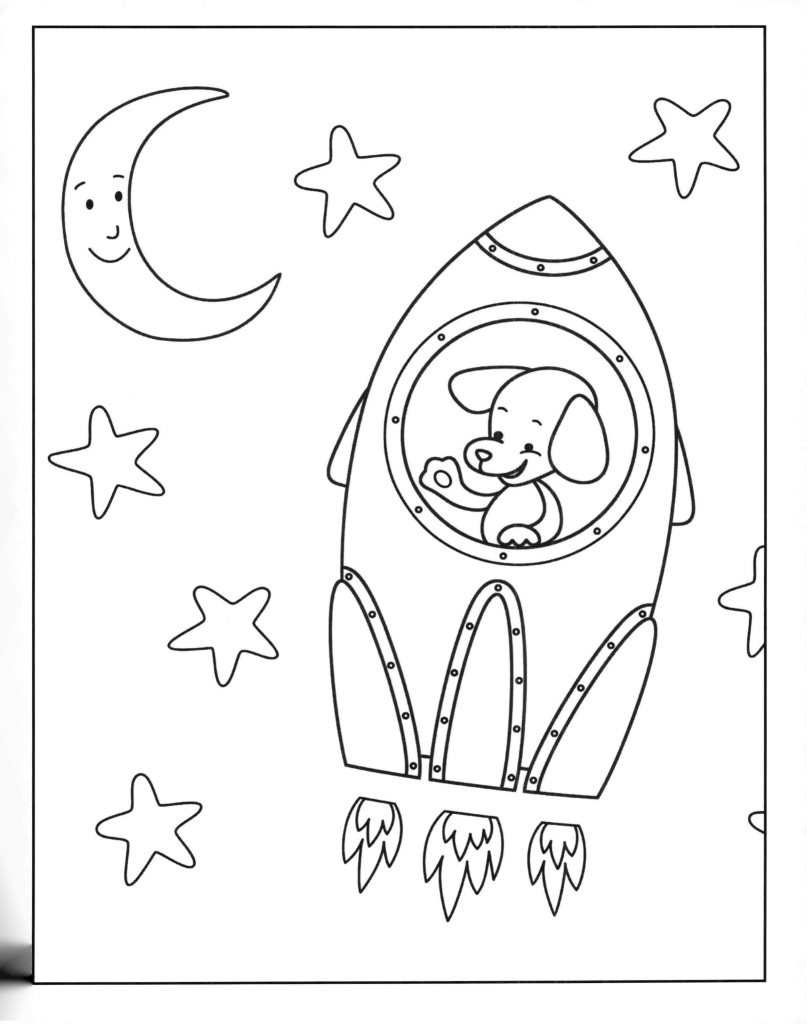

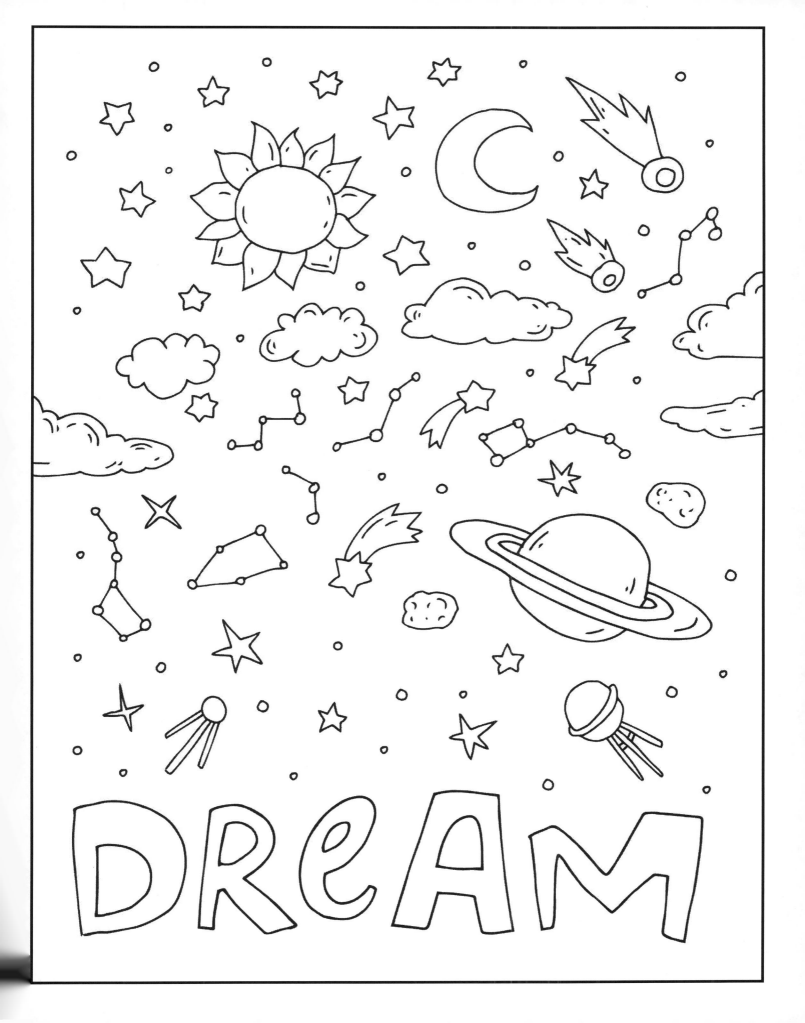

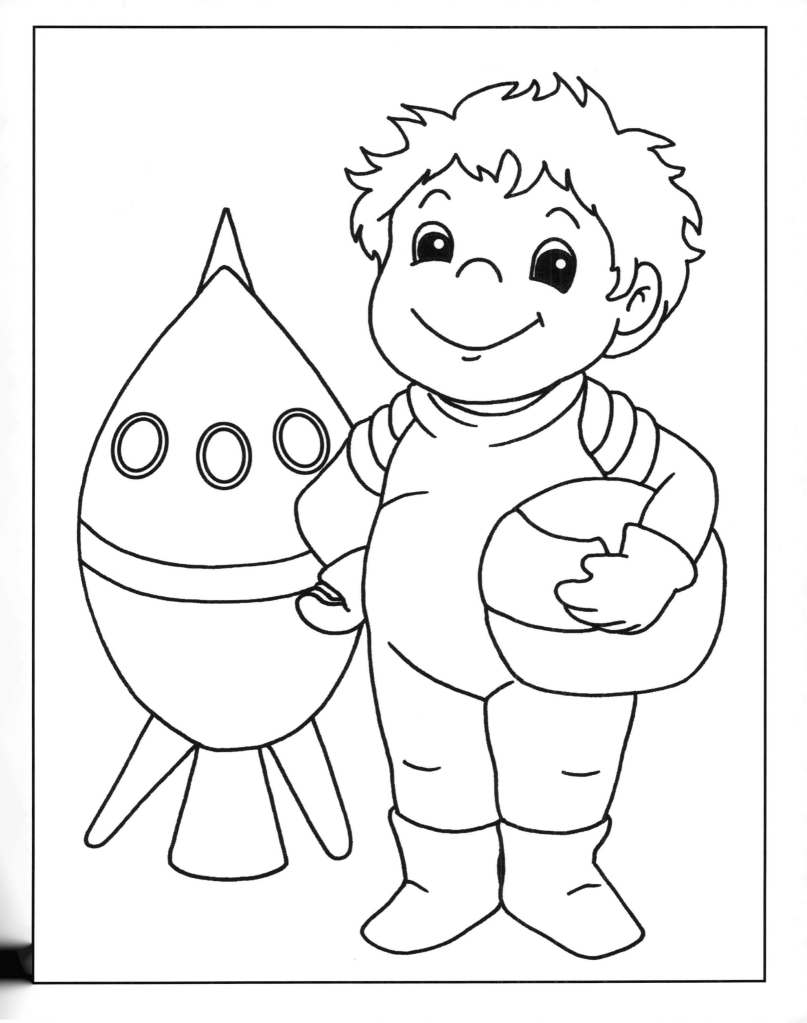

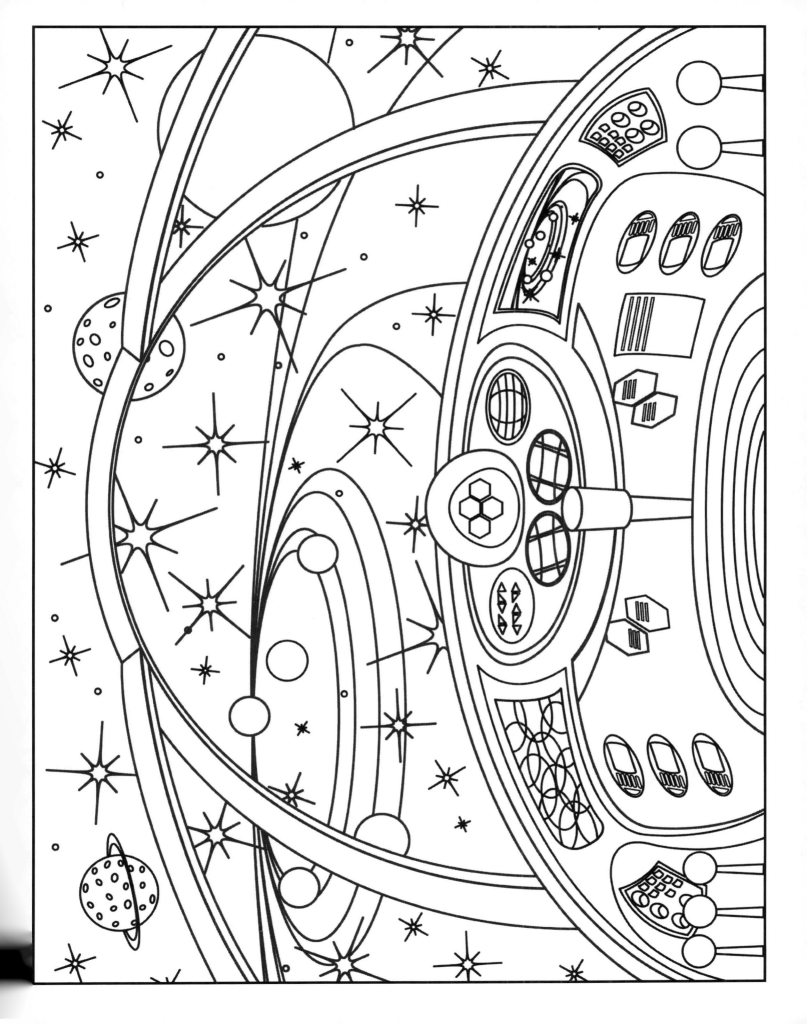

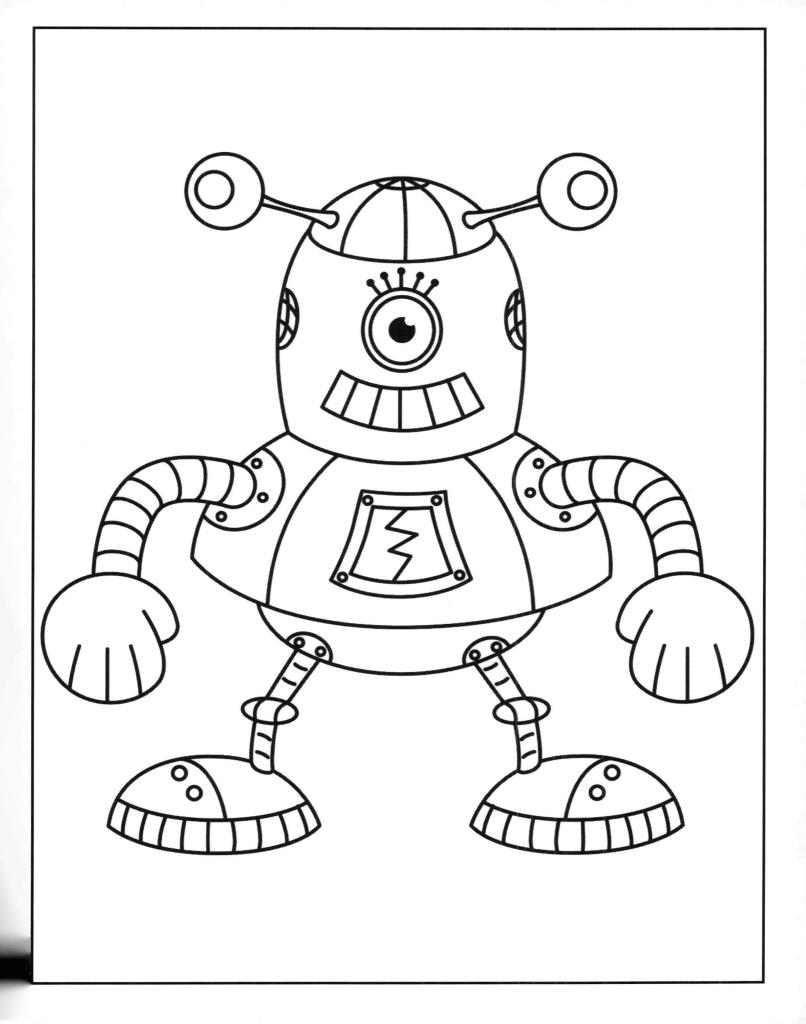

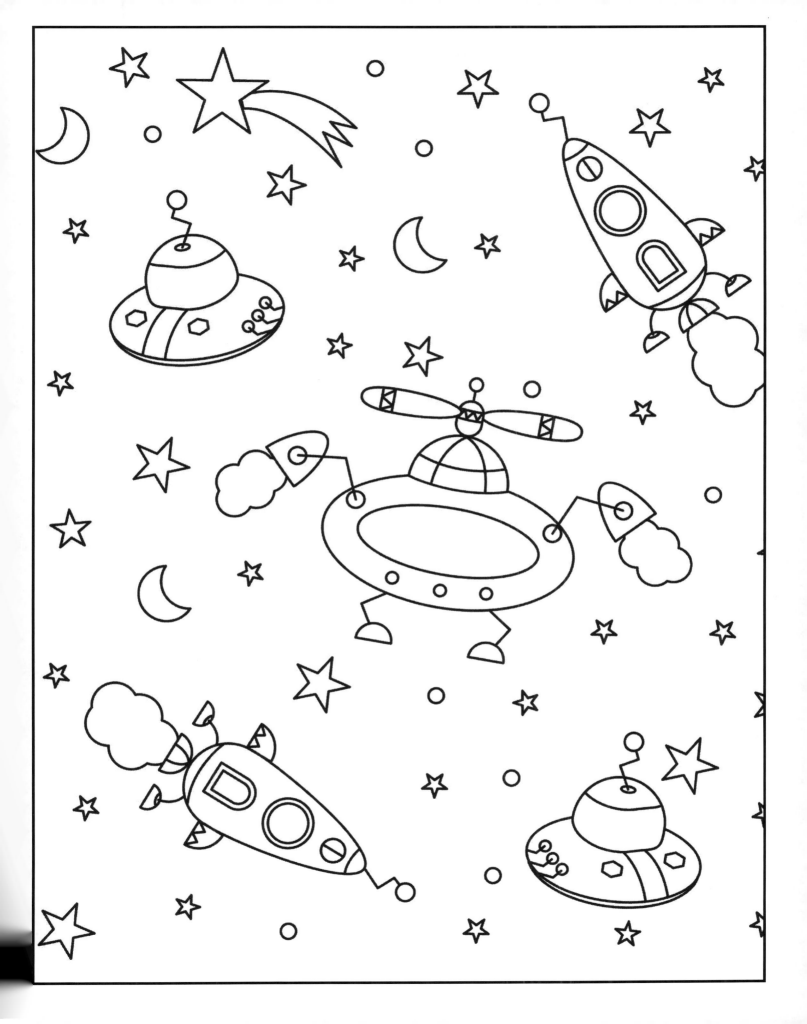

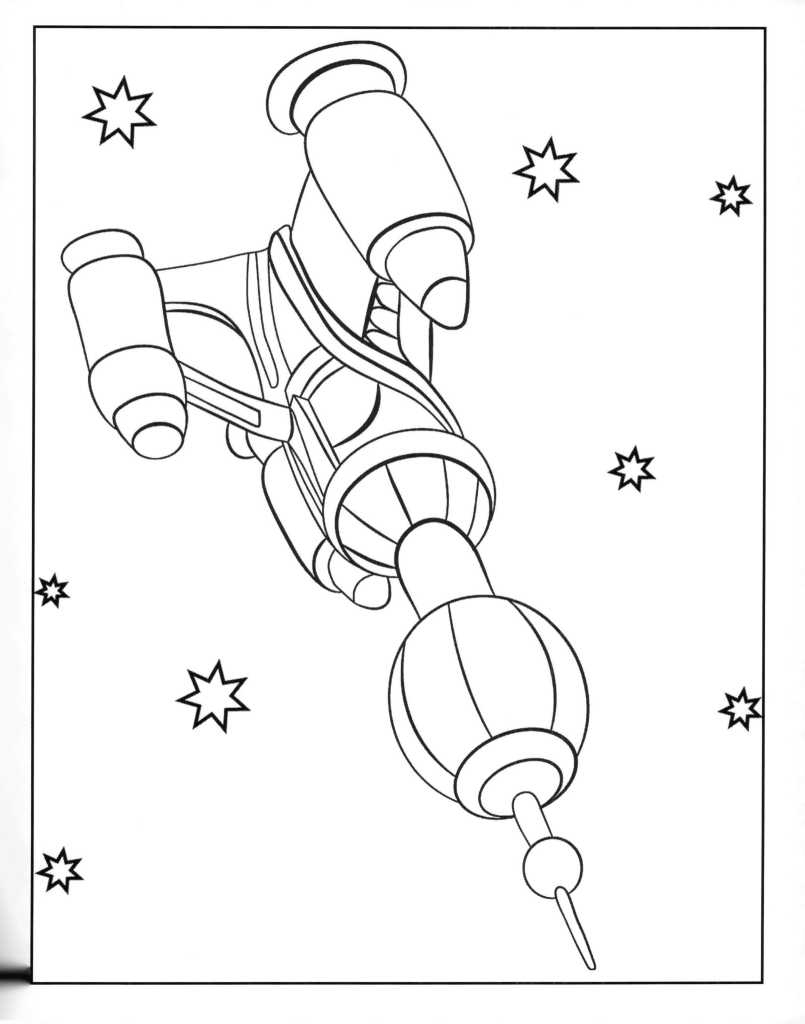

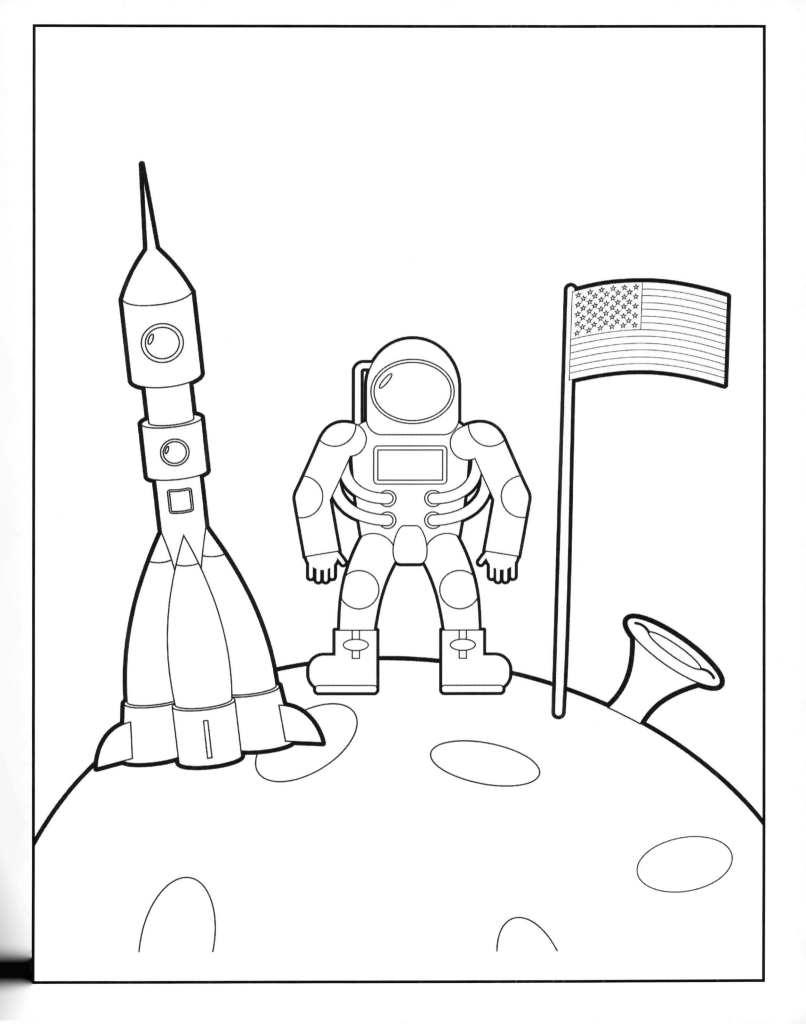

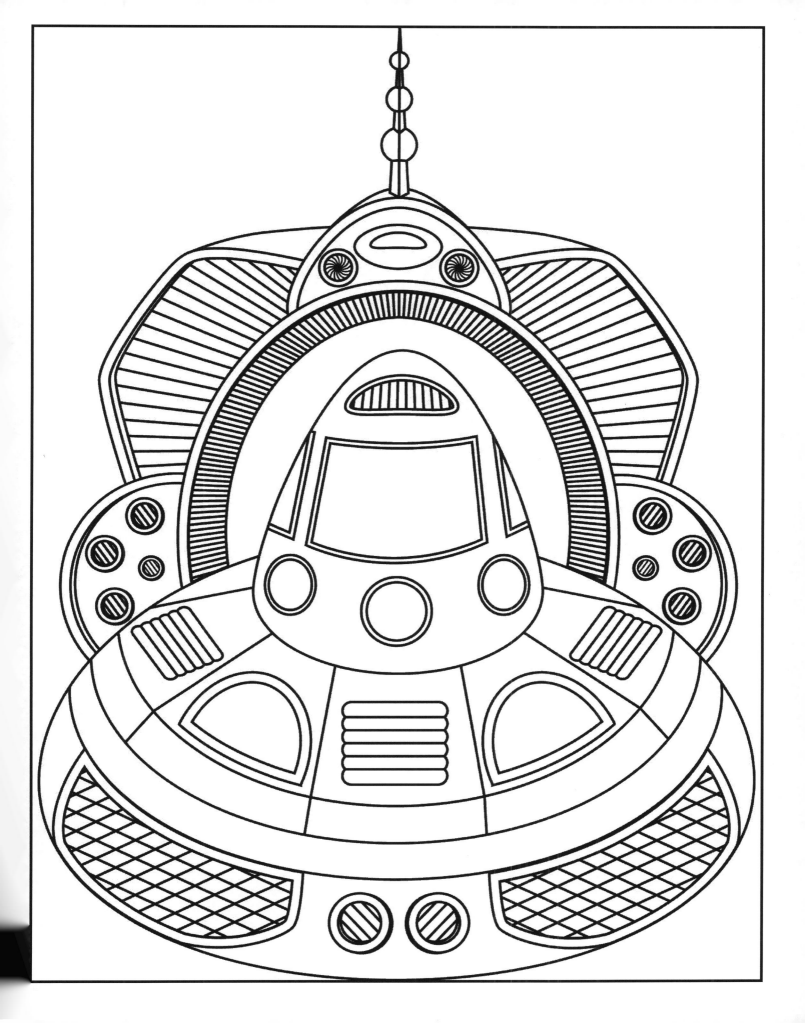

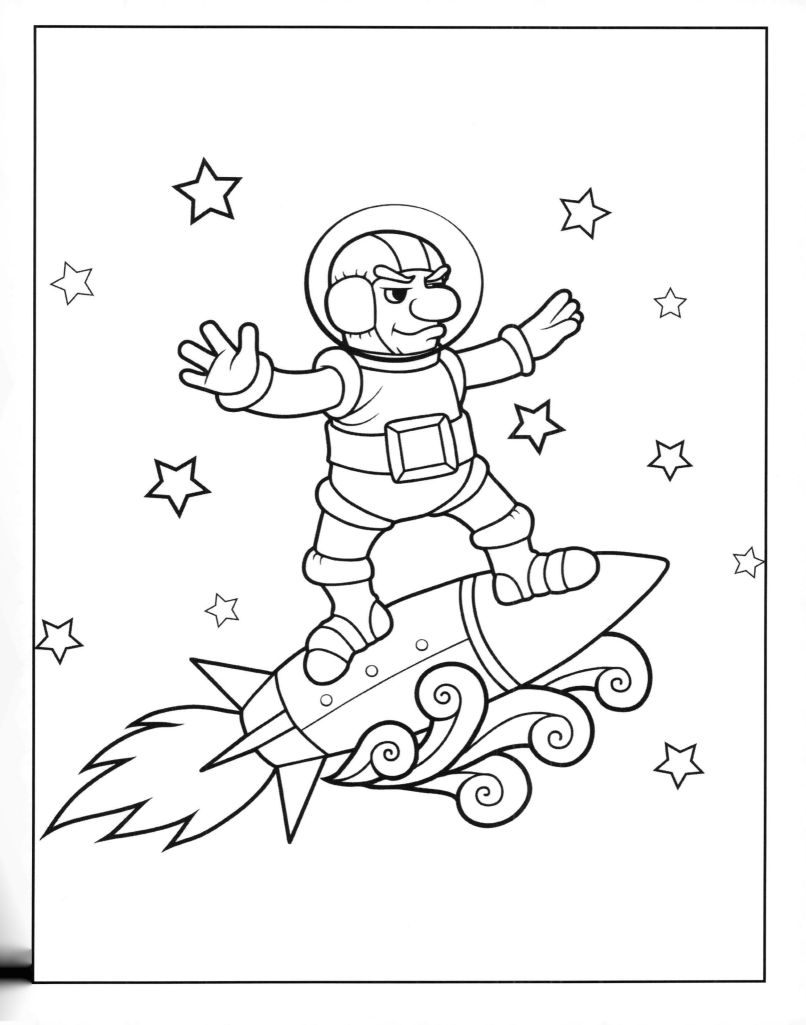

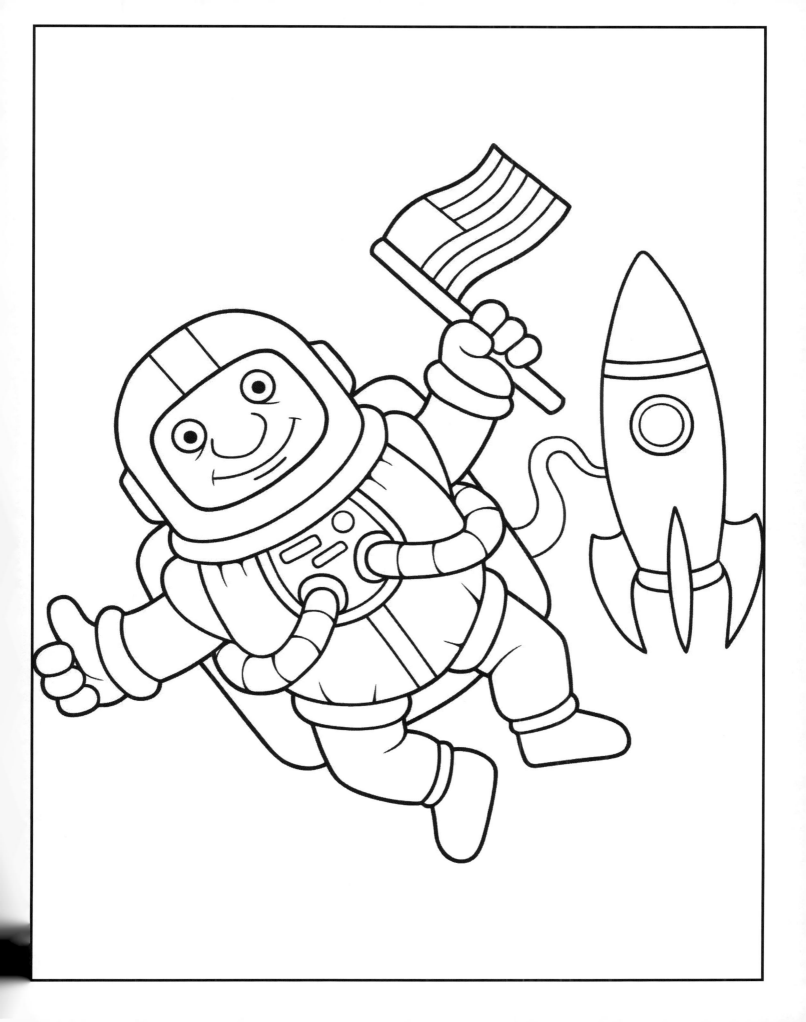

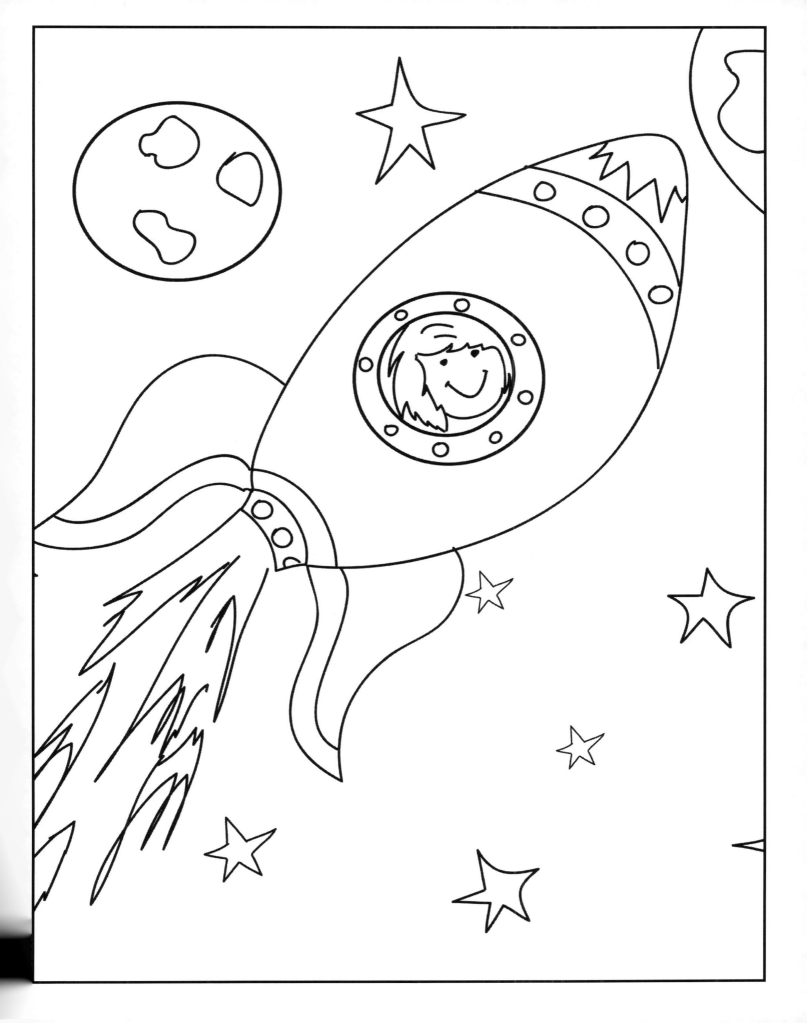

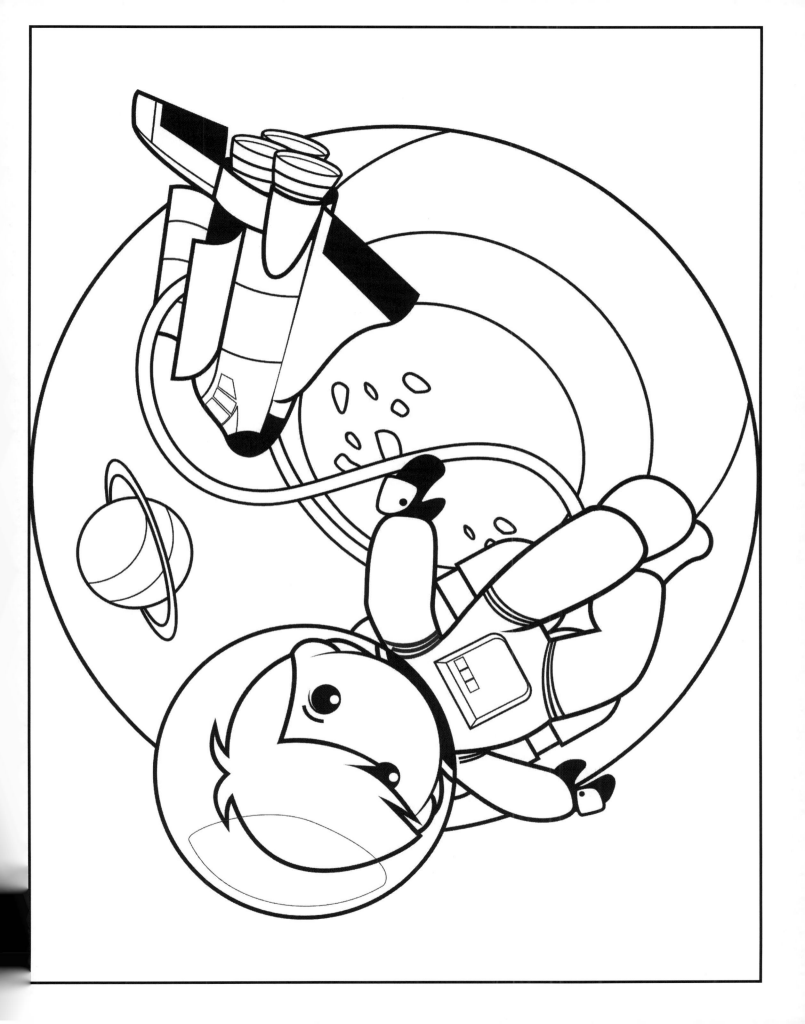

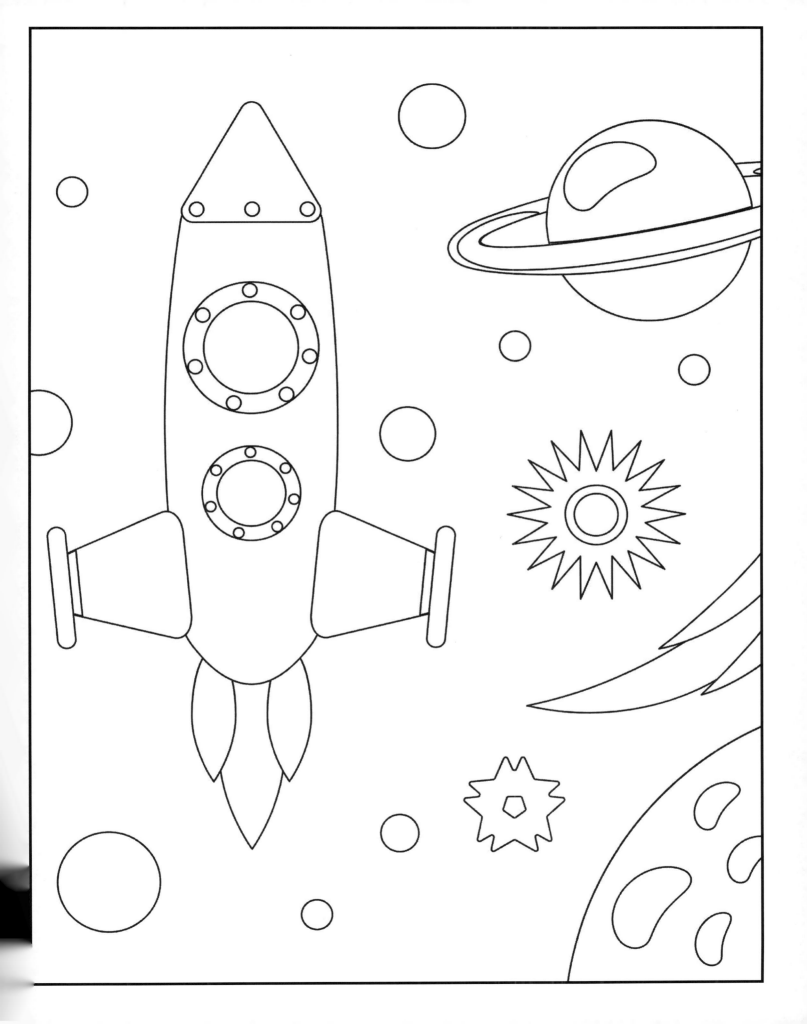

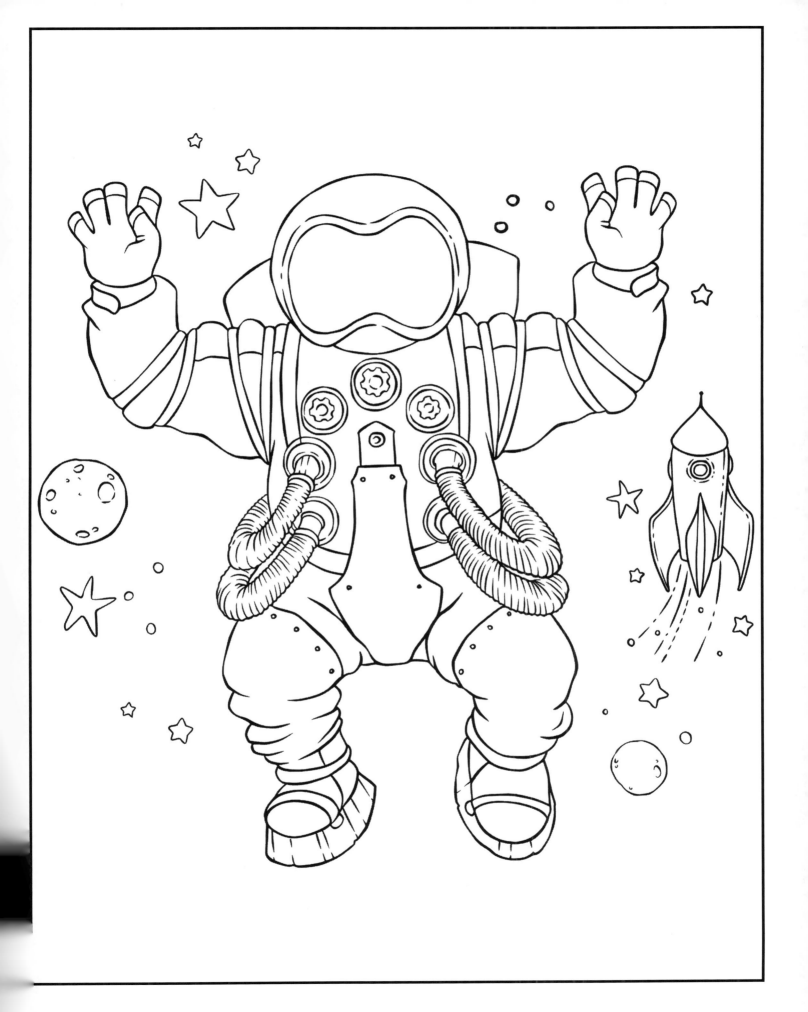

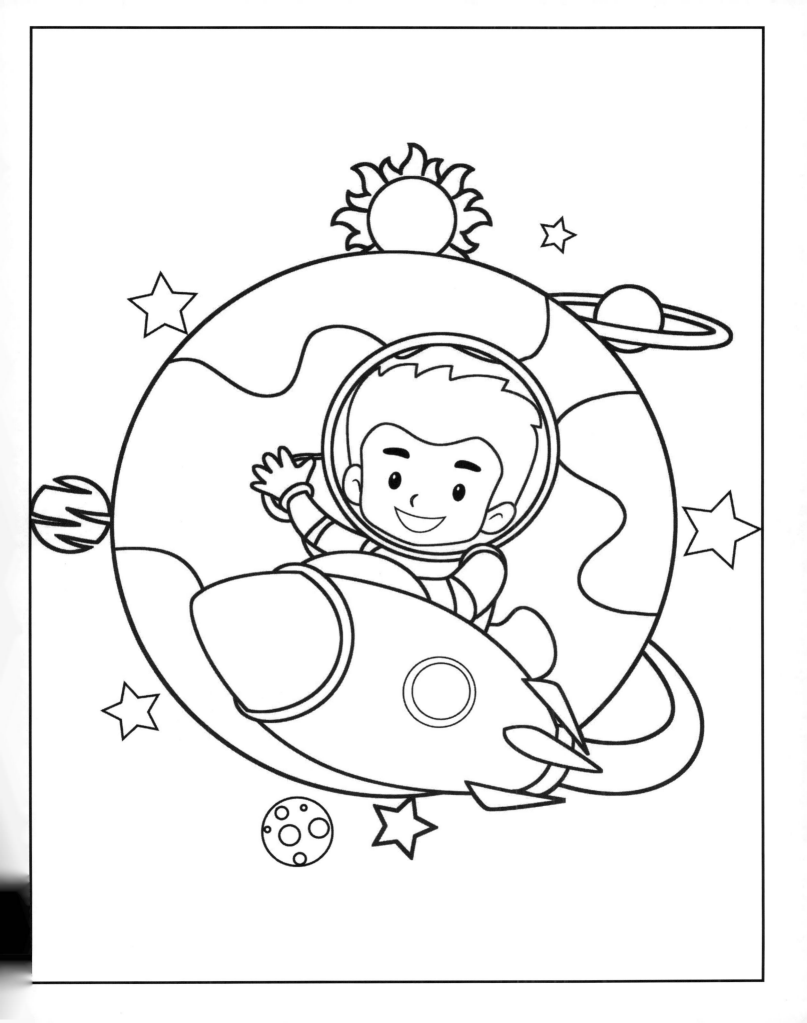

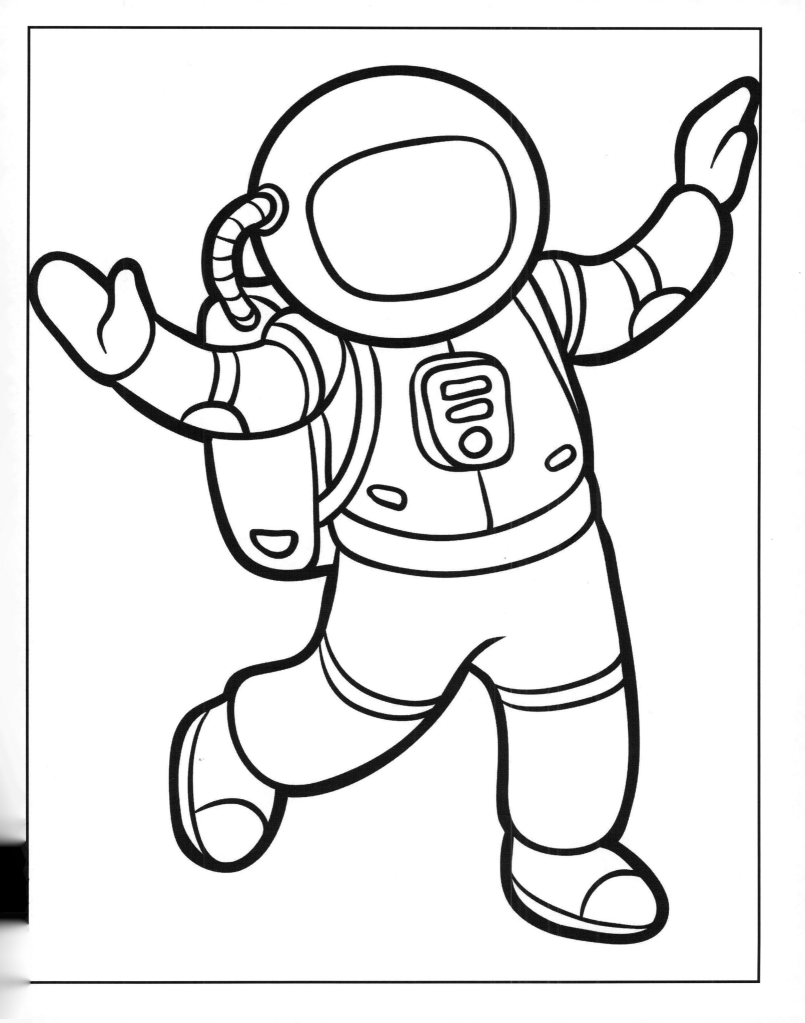

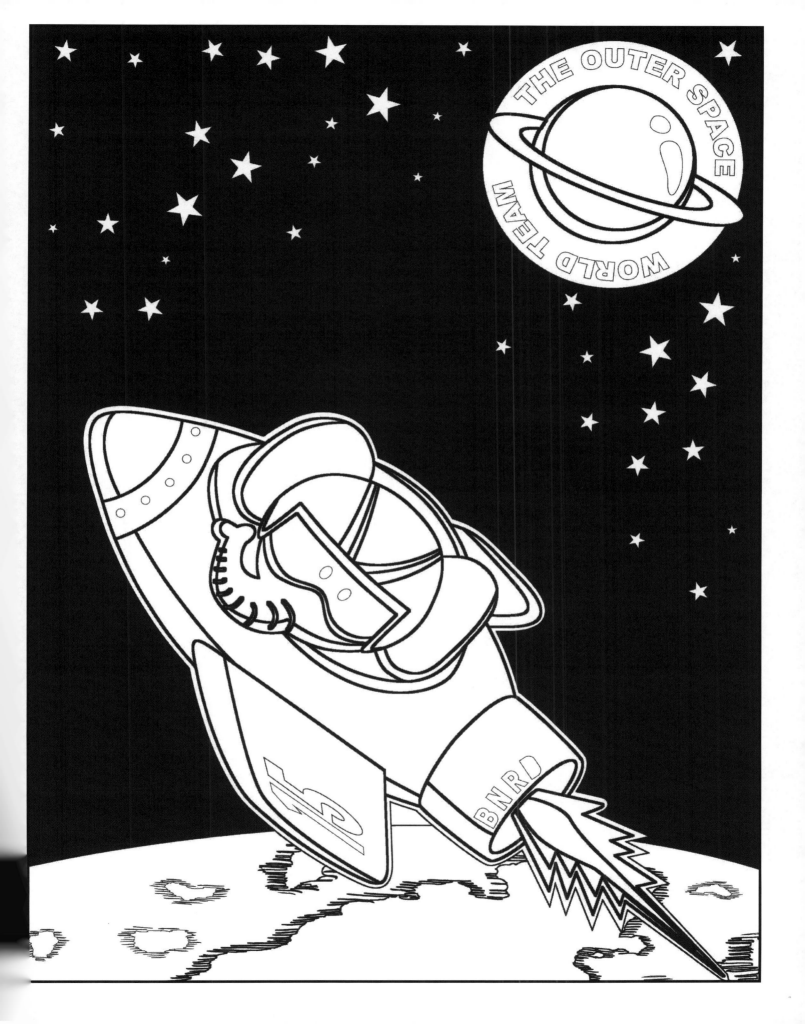

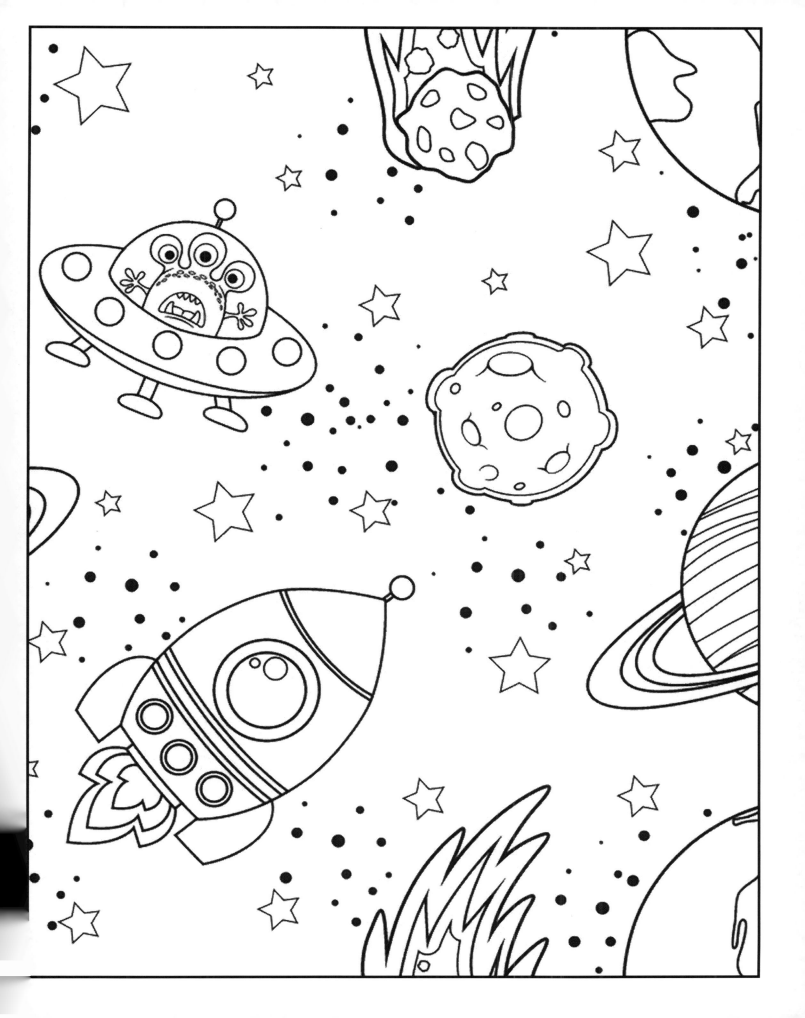

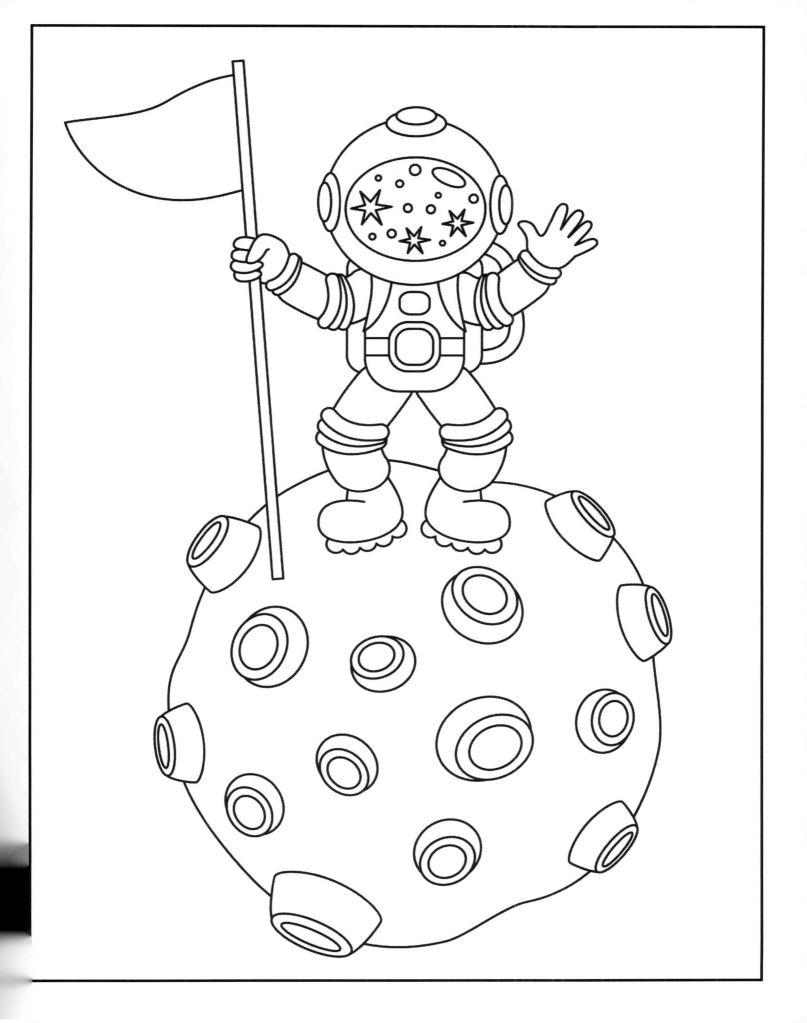

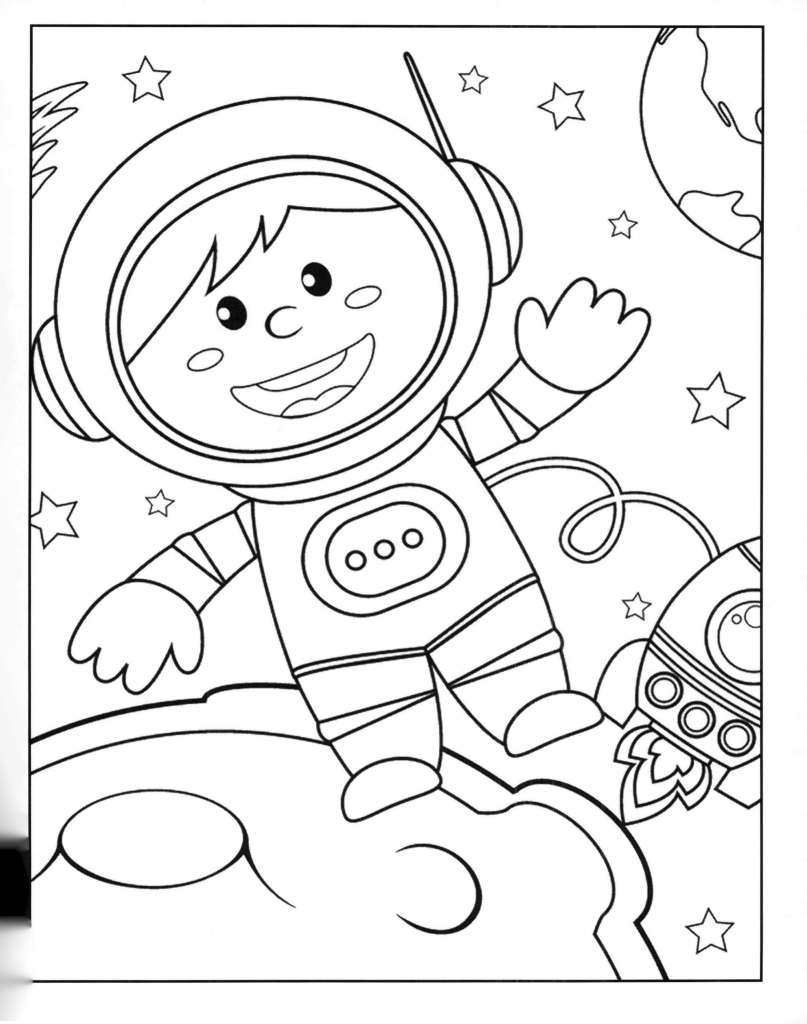

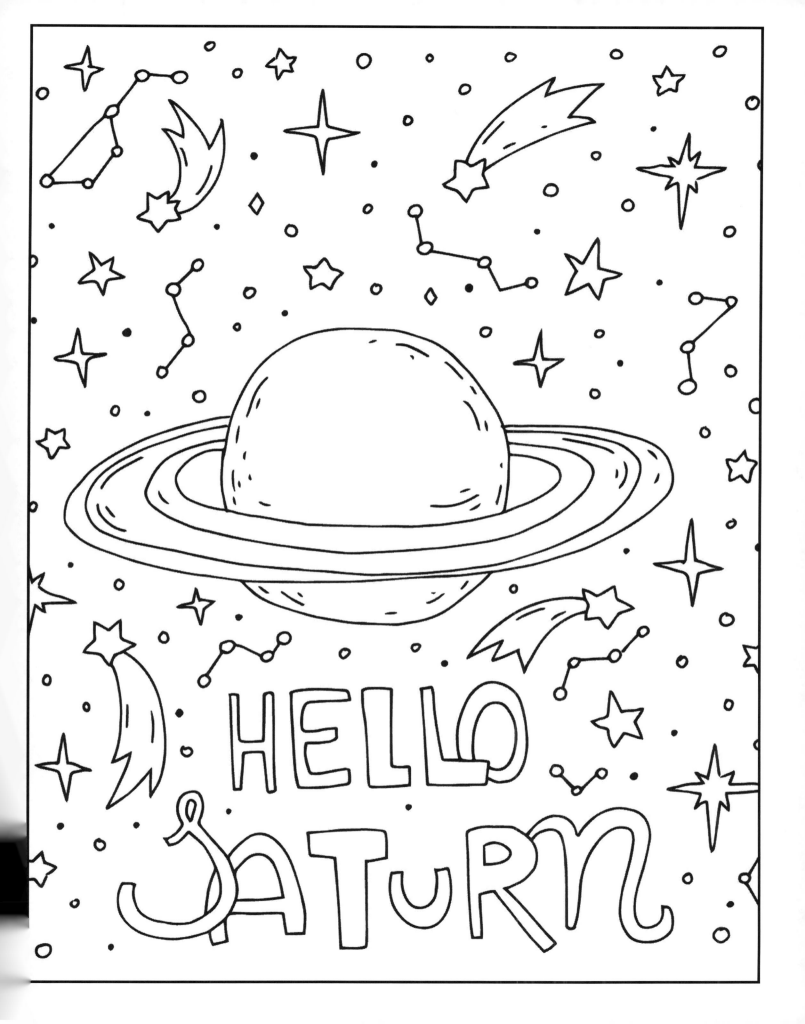

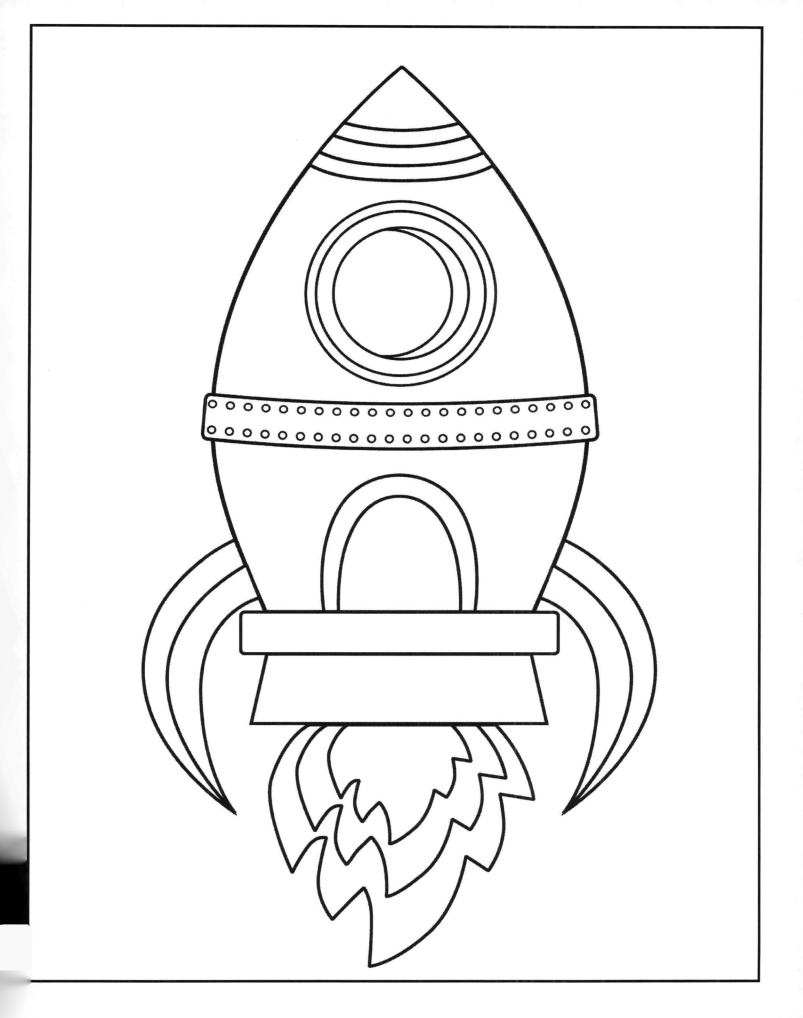

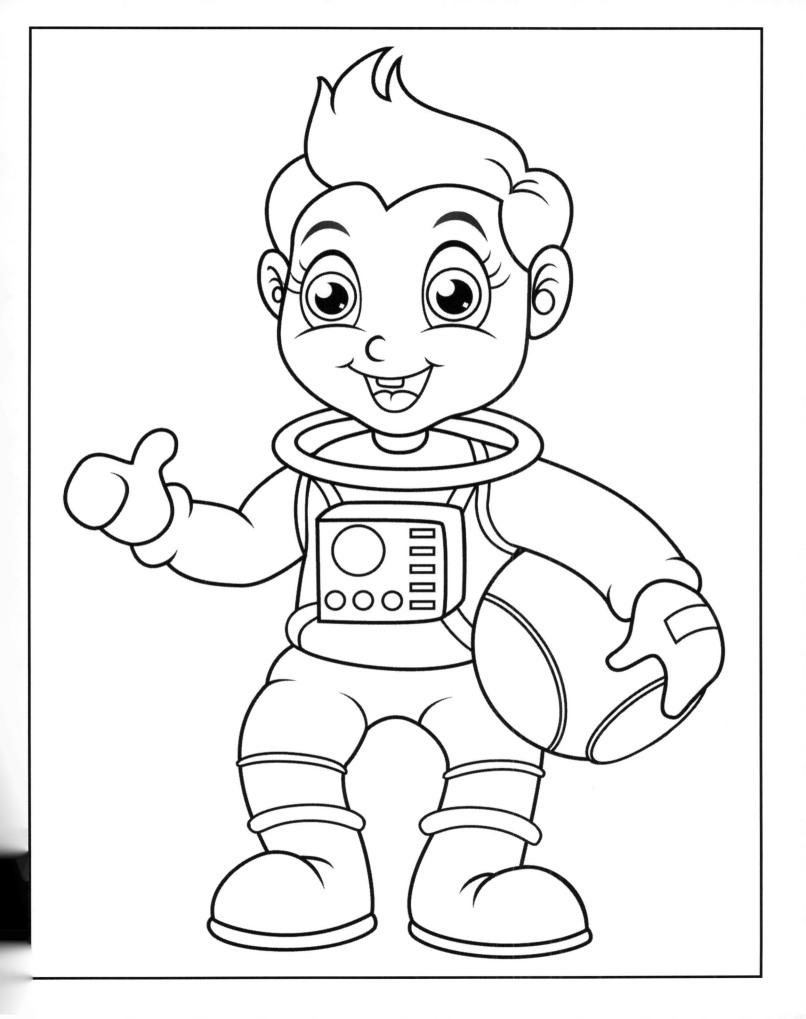

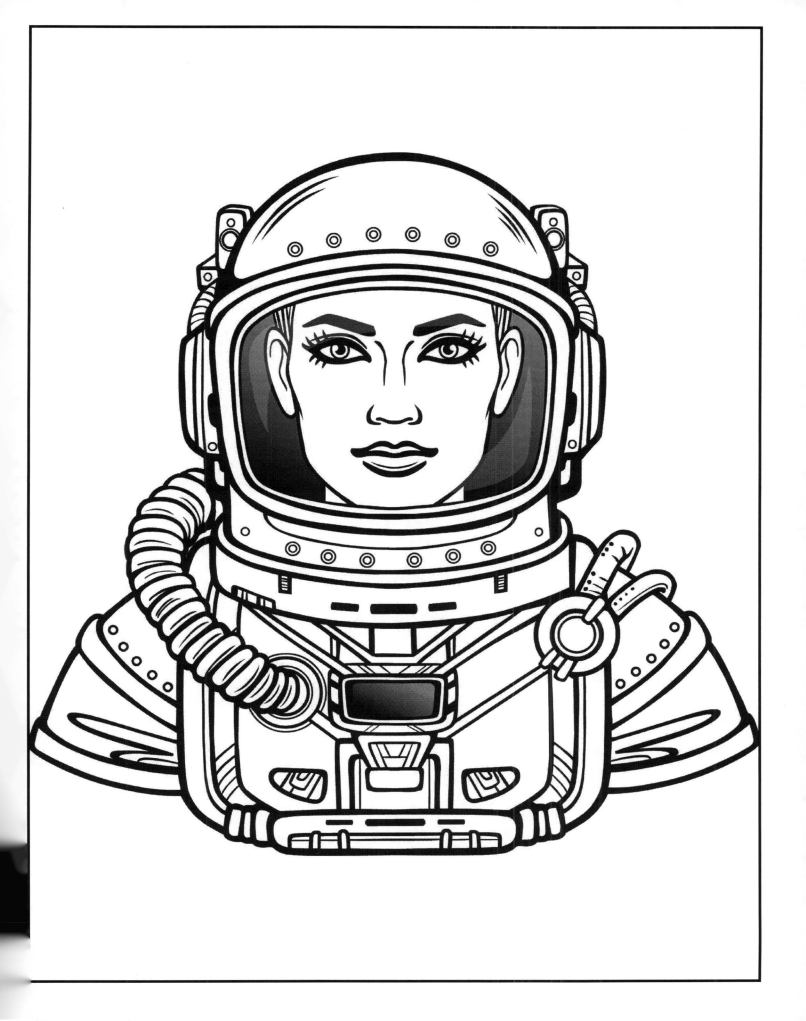

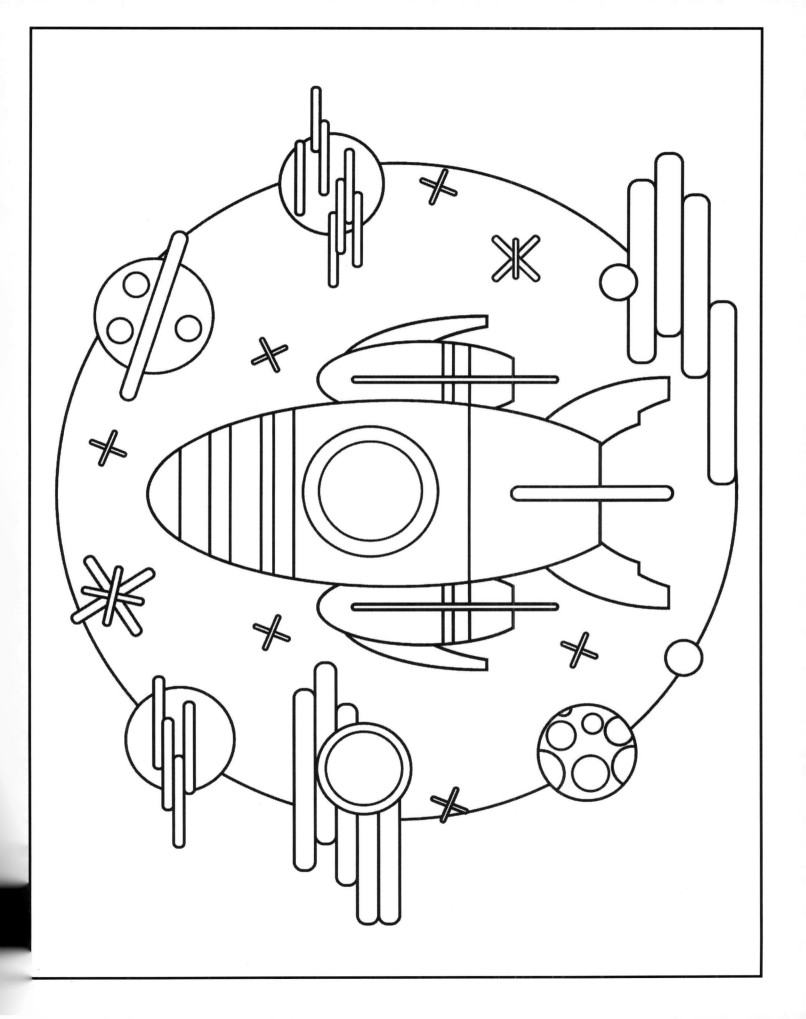

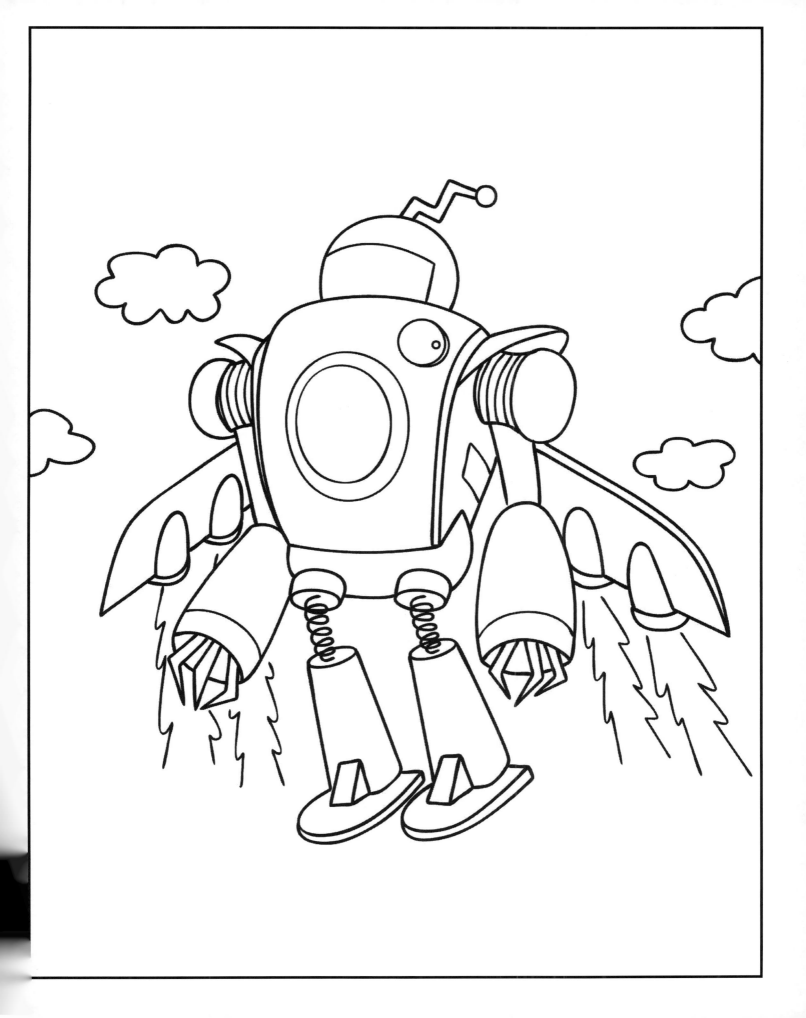

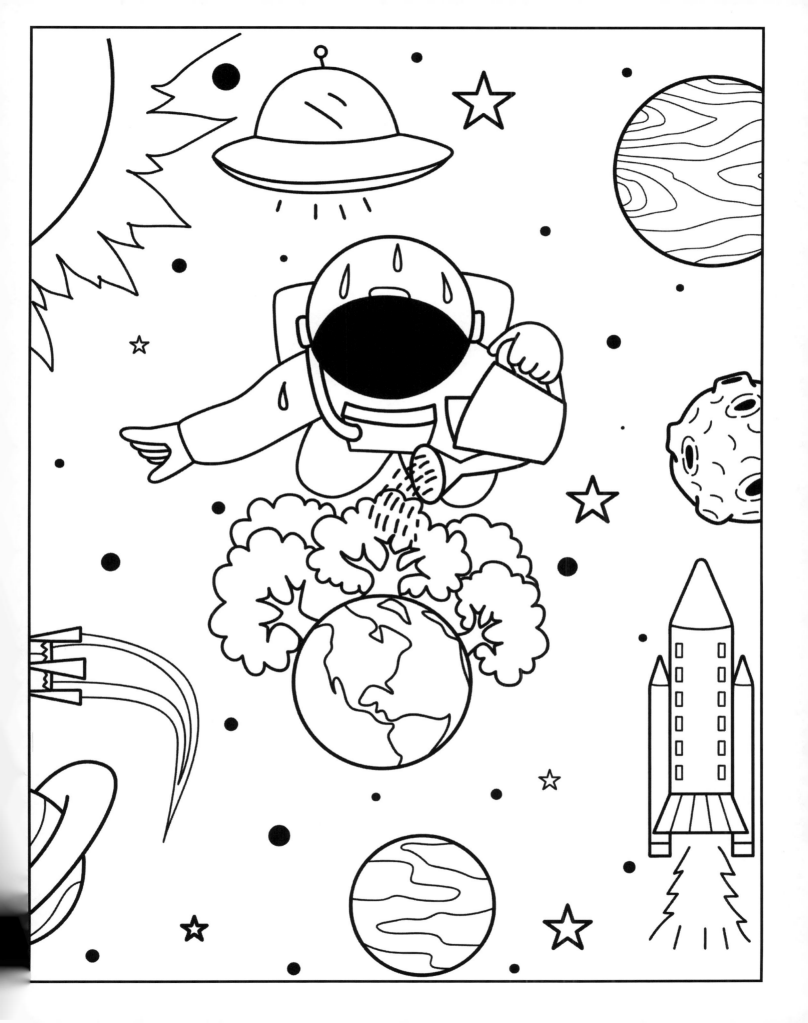

Bonus

Turn the page for bonus pages from some of our most popular coloring and activity books.

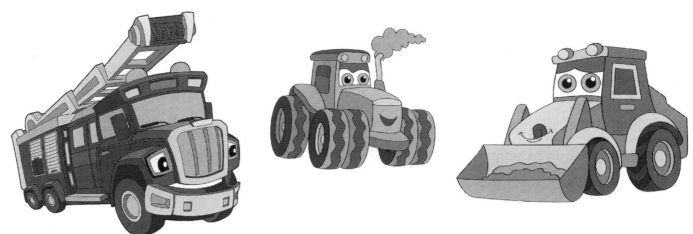

TRUCK
COLORING BOOK

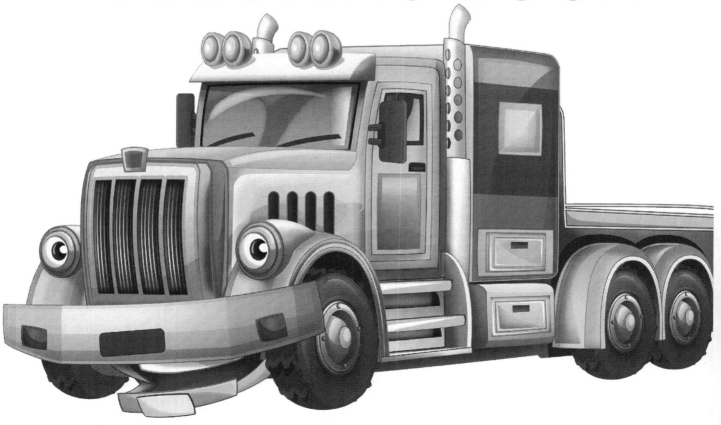

COLORING BOOKS FOR KIDS

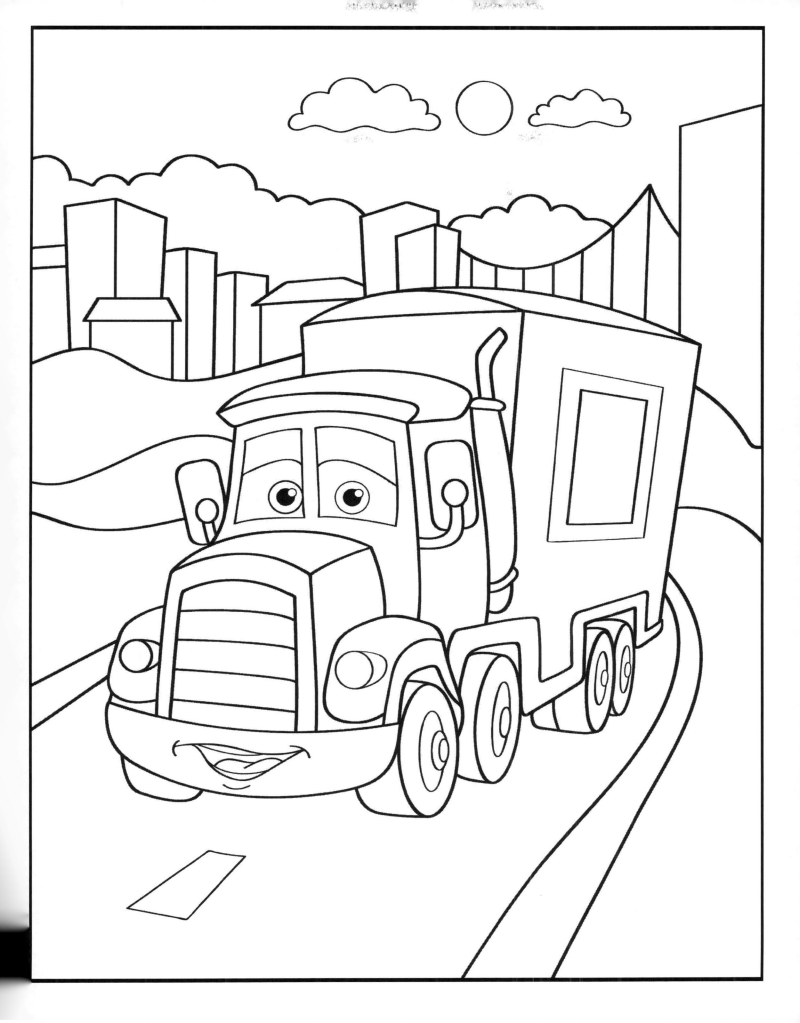

Connect the Dots
Book for Kids

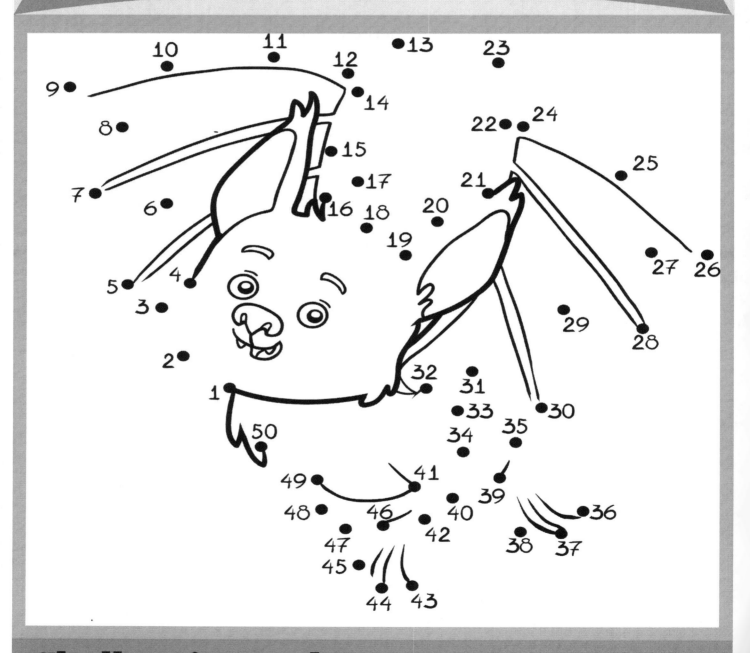

Challenging and Fun Dot to Dot Puzzles

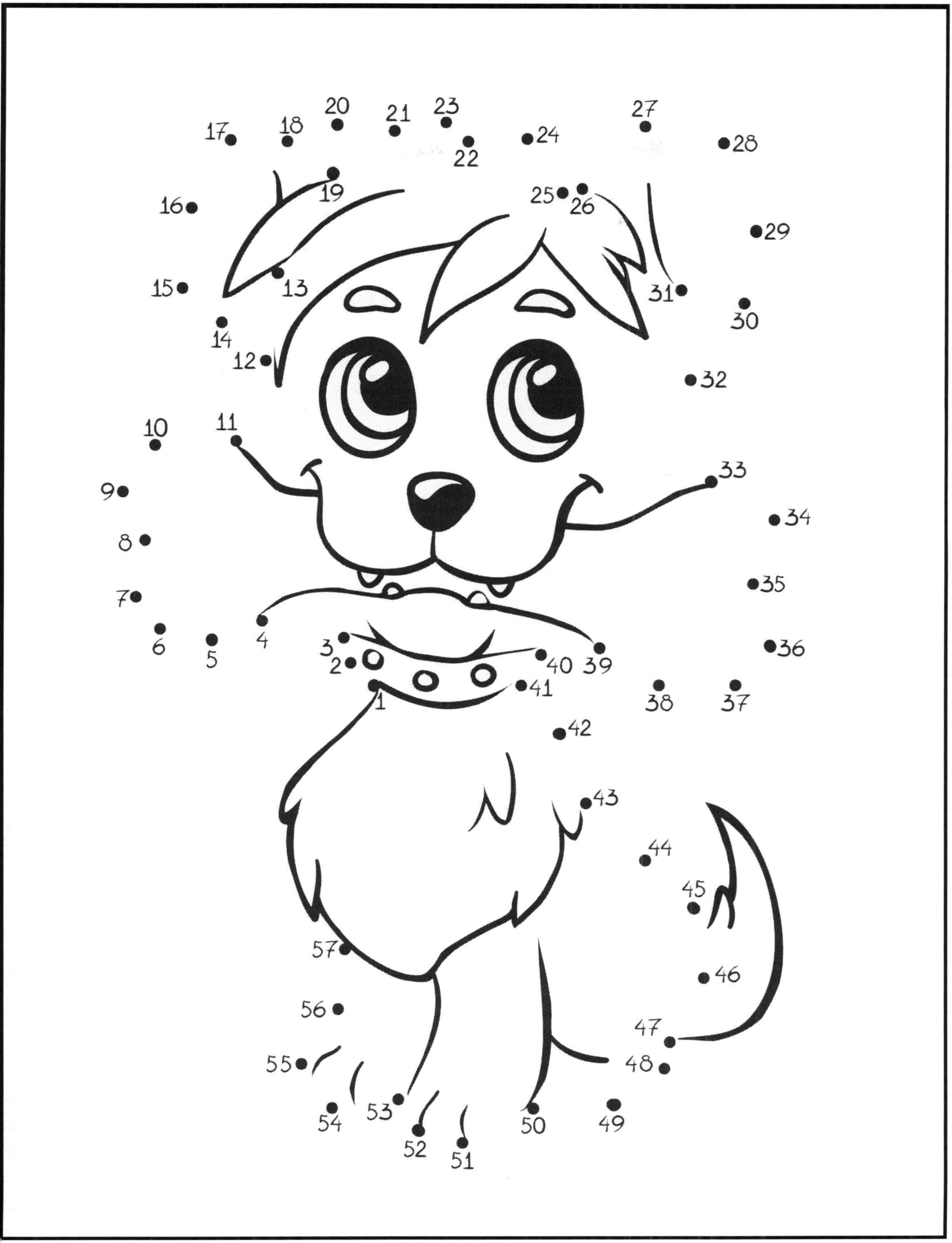
1
2
3
4
5
6
7
8
9
10
11
12
13
14
15
16
17
18
19
20
21
22
23
24
25
26
27
28
29
30
31
32
33
34
35
36
37
38
39
40
41
42
43
44
45
46
47
48
49
50
51
52
53
54
55
56
57

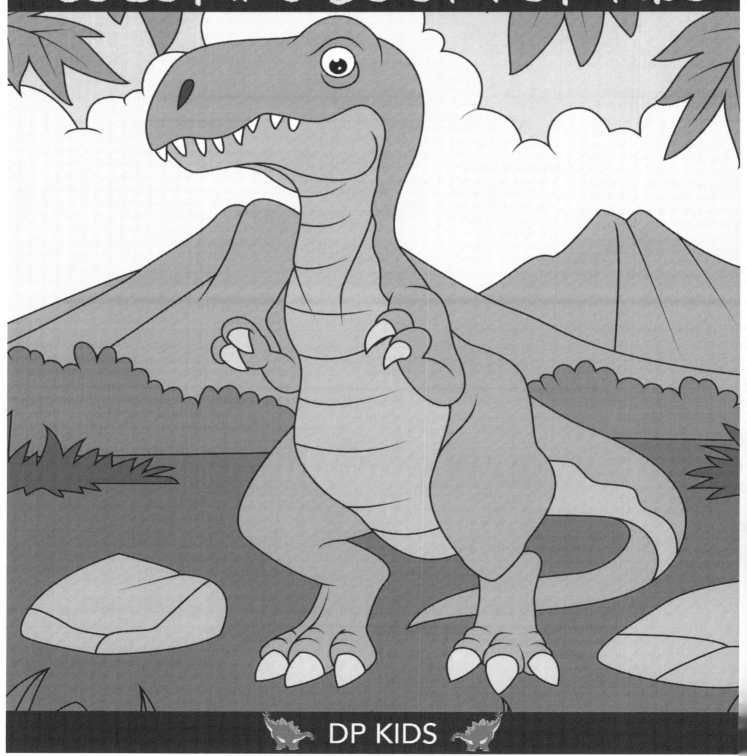

DINOSAUR
COLORING BOOK FOR KIDS

DP KIDS

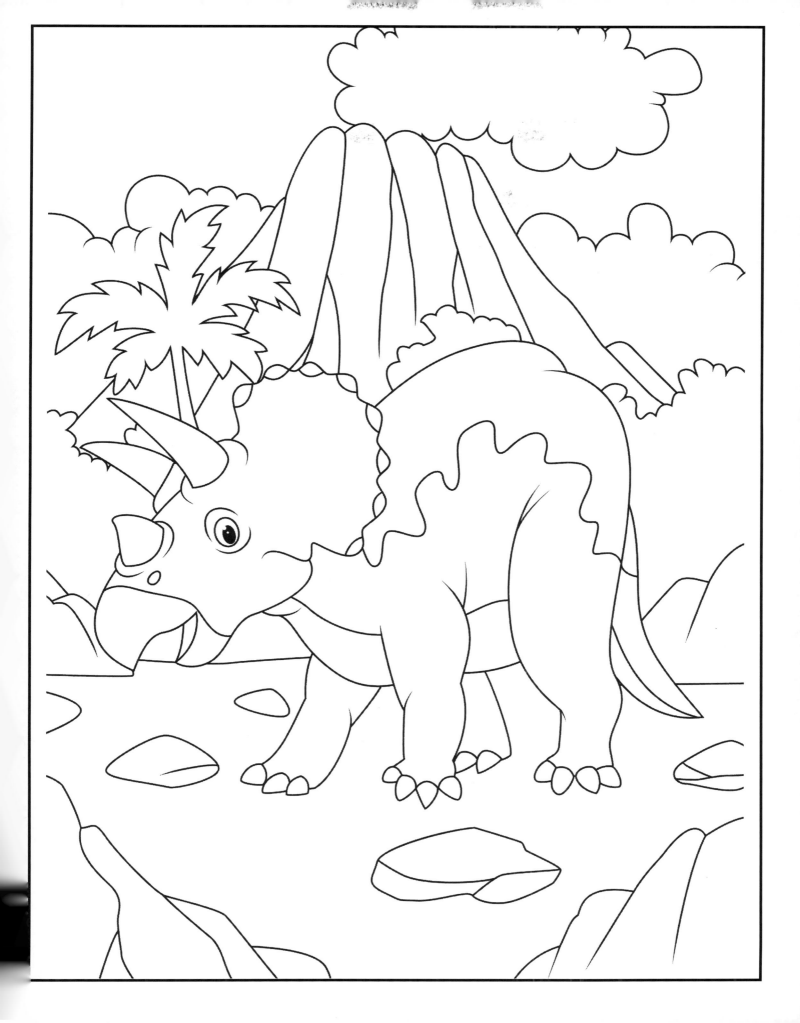